D1527076

are you experienced?

baby
boom
poets at
are you midlife

experienced?

EDITED BY PAMELA GEMIN

University of Iowa Press ψ Iowa City

University of Iowa Press, Iowa City 52242

Copyright © 2003 by the University of Iowa Press

All rights reserved

Printed in the United States of America

Text design by Richard Hendel

http://www.uiowa.edu/uiowapress

The publication of this book was generously supported
by the University of Iowa Foundation.

Printed on acid-free paper

Library of Congress Cataloging-in-Publication Data

Are you experienced? Baby Boom poets at midlife / edited by
Pamela Gemin.

    p.   cm.

Includes index.

ISBN 0-87745-850-2 (pbk.)

    1. American poetry—20th century. 2. Baby boom generation—Poetry.
3. Midlife crisis—Poetry. 4. Middle age—Poetry. I. Gemin, Pamela, 1954–.

PS595.B25 A74 2003

811′.5408—dc21   2002075077

03 04 05 06 07 P 5 4 3 2 1

This book is dedicated

to the memory of

ROSEANNE HOEFEL, 1962–2001

Forever Young

CONTENTS

III. WOVEN IN MY WALK

ACKNOWLEDGMENTS

Love and thanks to my family, Patricia and William Pierce and
Joseph Gemin, and to the friends and colleagues who continue to
support my endeavors with unconditional zeal, especially Sandy
Brucks, Kim Edwards, Eugene Haun, Marguerite Helmers, Charles Hill,
Julie King, Paul Klemp, Jane Kramer, Estella Lauter, Jan Norton, John
Reinhard, Ron Rindo, Rich Rummel, Sue Rummel, and Ellen Shriner.
Warm gratitude to the poets and mentors David Graham, Betsy Sholl,
and Kate Sontag for their insights and critical input. Blessings upon
Jeanine Burns, who typed most of these poems, and Guy Witzel, whose
keen eye assured that they remained true to form. I am especially
grateful to Paula Sergi for her valuable editorial assistance and to Holly
Carver, Megan Scott, Charlotte Wright, and all at the University of Iowa
Press, who once again worked their magic to bring so many important
voices together under one cover.

"If a lifetime is North America then I have reached Kansas," declares
Diane Seuss in a poem honoring the advent of midlife, the ill-fitting shoes
of childhood cast off with the shackles of love while "Joe the Reaper,
a sweet slack-jawed / boy who's too good at his work," slides on ahead.
"From here," she says, we can "see it all coming." Arriving on hindsight's
heels, midlife's insights are startling, and who better than poets to deliver
them? As these poems gathered, they revealed a striking variety of sub-
jects for which midlife served as a vantage point. One poem at a time,
a chorus of voices assembled itself, voices in a common range, bringing
stories of a second coming of age.

I was surprised that some poets were reluctant to be classified as "mid-
lifers," yet pending any medical breakthroughs, a person born in the
middle of the Baby Boom—let's say a few years on either side of 1954, the
year of my birth—probably won't live another forty-nine years. That's OK
with me. That's how it's supposed to go, the way it is designed. When my
friend's twenty-one-year-old daughter rolls her eyes at her mother and
me, we remind ourselves that eye-rolling at oldsters is *her* job now. When
my college students' music fails to stir up anything inside me but a lather
of annoyance, or when I flick through the channels and find myself
repelled yet creepily fascinated by MTV's *Real World*, I know that things
are indeed progressing as they should, and I am strangely comforted. The
girl in the paisley kerchief whining about "Brandon's issues with inti-
macy" is, thank God, not me, though I wore that same kerchief to a Led
Zeppelin concert, with a suede vest whose fringe hung almost to the floor.
My long-abandoned vest is a lucky someone's Halloween costume. I could
no longer button it, or zip up my silver satin pants, or walk more than a
few steps in my matching platforms without my arches collapsing. My
coolness has gone the way of all coolness, my hipness the way of all hip-
ness, lost in the high cost of maintenance and surrendered to those whose
job it is now to be cool and hip.

Are you experienced?—that ambiguous, electric, open-ended question
of our youth finds an answer here, in this collection of poems: yes, yes,
yes. Grown up, sold out, burned out, red with insomniac rust, faithful, dis-
illusioned, hopeful, resurrected, shining.

To a generation that sought to stay forever young in spirit and in pur-
pose, midlife should mean more than suffering jokes about thinning hair,
creaking joints, and thickening waistlines, though the poets here have

much to say about the waning of physical power, the onset of serious illness, and the ever changing map of the body. Just getting "a good fix on time," as Stephen Dunn says, is task enough, let alone understanding what Alison Townsend calls "time's sweet and invincible secret: / that everything repeats." Some poets, like Ann Hostetler, revisit their youthful desires: "I wanted to be a priestess of love," she confesses, "angel of mercy, crystal in a sun-streaked window," the kind of groovy love child Bill Bauer lusted after in "Wildflowers," who led him past "no trespassing signs on deserted farms . . . barefoot into new gardens." In a previous incarnation, these lovers take on the shades of parents who may have created them, the mother and father dancing to Ray Charles and Patsy Cline in Bob Hicok's "Choosing My Conception."

In poets' memories of home, poems move like ghosts through old houses, neighborhoods, and bars. Children crawl out of their grown-up shadows to mourn vanishing landscapes. "I want to curl inside a sidewalk square / my ear to the ground . . . what could I bring / back to life?" asks Jim Daniels's speaker in "Blessing the House." "When I come / To where our house was, / I come to weeds," says Gary Soto of his childhood home on Braly Street. "Where the almond tree stood / There are wine bottles." In "Thoreau," Timothy Liu's father and son are exiled to a curb by the father's wife, who fears she might contract AIDS from being near them. In their moment of mutual displacement, father and son mourn separate losses: the orchards of the father's childhood "are gone, his village near Shanghai / bombed . . ," while the son remembers the trees of his own lifetime, "apricot, / walnut, peach, and plum—hacked down."

The complexity of family life evolves for those midlife Baby Boomers who face the demands of raising children while remaining accessible to aging parents. In the same wrinkle of time, they might be reading aloud at a mother's bedside or home worrying about a teenage daughter like the one in Betsy Sholl's "Chances," who "will turn the barker's heads / with her yellow hair, as she goes to test / night's loud music and chintzy lights." Some may find themselves blending into brand-new families, as in Kate Sontag's "Making Step Beautiful in Maine," or mapping out a new "Geography of Love" in a midlife adoption, as in Laurel Mills's poem about an orphaned godson dropped like a falling star into the home of a midlife lesbian couple.

As new bonds form, old ones weaken, break, or repair, and love always comes back looking for us—persuaded by what Yusef Komunyakaa calls "the fat juice / of promises"—through heartbreak, social disdain, divorce, disillusion, and even death. "Love was the ghost whose shape kept / shifting," says Rebecca McClanahan in "Making Love," while Deborah Keenan calls it a "complicated and beautiful circle." For Kel Munger's couple, loving "[i]n another city, another state . . . might be a crime." And deep into their marriage, "snuggled under thistles and nettles," Ronald Wallace's partners find the wild strawberries "so fragile and ripe / their own weight in the bowl could ruin or bruise them."

As the poets here venture into the territory of excess and addiction, they rattle up their own demons. "[W]e drank the river / nearly to its bed at times, and were so numb / . . . all pain / was pleasant since that's all there was, pain, / and everything that was deeply felt, deeply / was not . . . ," Thomas Lux recalls in "Loudmouth Soup." Racism, violence, political corruption, war wounds, and environmental blundering are also alive and well in their poems. "We're just fine—look at the way / everyone wants to speak English and live here!" declares the "Exquisite Candidate" created by Denise Duhamel and Maureen Seaton, as buildings implode and children assassinate other children. Bruce Jacobs's persona struggles with his own racial misconceptions in "Black on Black," and David Wojahn's animal handlers collect the sperm that might save his kind from Rajah, one of the world's four thousand remaining tigers. The Great Boomer Sellout is acknowledged in poems like Martín Espada's ironic take on an upscale restaurant and Marcia Southwick's melancholy assessment of the news. And poets such as Lisa Lewis, Holly Iglesias, and Tony Hoagland appraise the next generation with ironic humor.

And there is still a treasure of faith to be found in these pages. God arrives in the form of an owl in Martín Espada's housing project, "a solemn white bird bending the curtain rod," his image bathed in the "cackling glow of the television." Forgiveness is granted, candles are lit, saints glow on dashboards, and dogs howl at the moon. And though, like the Vietnam vet in Bruce Weigl's poem, "[w]e are not always right / about what we think will save us," Laura Kasischke's love letter to Earth might serve as a blessing rained upon the second half of life: "The view / from here is too removed, diluted. . . . I want / to fall all over you like a farm, to bless / your fields with weeping. . . . My / tornadoes tearing up your prairies. My / red wind licking its initials in the dust." Sounds like Kansas, all right.

PAMELA GEMIN

In this book, you will encounter a good deal of news that has stayed news for centuries: the great themes of lyric poetry are stubbornly persistent. Sappho or Li Po would agree, as the poets collected here do, that life is a hot dream, briefer, it often seems, than a summer storm; that the sweetness of love can come to us like grace, sudden, odd, and unstoppable; that nothing good arrives without its accompanying shadow of loss—along with the ache of such recognition; that memory both preserves and rein-vents the past; that the blood pull of kinship in its many forms is our tragic and, at times, comic destiny; that doubt and faith form two sides of the same coin; that time is the ultimate mystery. These are some of the songs we cannot help singing, age after age, despite our frailty and despair, regardless of local circumstance.

Each age must reimagine and fashion its own versions of these pro-found and ordinary truths, just as each era must translate the classics to its own taste. The familiar is notoriously hard to see, much less express vividly, but we have little choice but to make the attempt—as this anthol-ogy does in setting out to chart the play of familiar lyric motifs within the compass of a single, highly storied generation at midlife.

It is always a matter of taste, of course—personal and, in the case of this book, also generational. Since Baby Boom poets share a range of ref-erence and experience, readers of a certain age will be forcibly struck by many details in this collection, by frequent references to rock and roll, drugs, Vietnam, the sexual revolution, and other formative features of our collective history. Midlife being a time of reckoning, poem after poem here reckons with love lost and gained, the aging of body and soul, the twists and turns of memory, and so on—all in the context of Baby Boom history.

But rather than focusing here on a generational definition, I want to at-tend to the editor's taste in another aspect, the poets' relish for the minute particulars of experience, the fragrance and swirl of life vividly rendered. By and large, this book collects poems that are, in Czeslaw Milosz's beau-tiful phrase, "loyal toward reality." William Carlos Williams once defined "the poet's business" as follows: "Not to talk in vague categories but to write particularly, as a physician works, upon a patient, upon the thing be-fore him, in the particular to discover the universal." Some would define the task of a poet more broadly (and some more narrowly), but the Williams tradition in our country has proved both fertile and durable.

Through the decades, a great deal of "talk in vague categories," as well as a certain portion of useful analysis, has indeed been committed by and about the Baby Boom generation. In this book, however, you will not find much abstraction. Mostly, you will find the stuff of life itself, as understood and expressed by the participants and as embodied in savory figure and image. And that is this book's special contribution, I think.

Ultimately, all that we know comes to us via the senses; and when skill-fully captured, the texture of experience is a pleasure in itself. Yet as William Carlos Williams knew well, such texture is also a window into all sorts of knowledge, and thus comprises both means and end. Poets who give us their accurate and fresh renditions, then, participate in an evergreen and necessary process. Poetic texture, as I am thinking of it, is more than decorative, more than a way of dressing up opinion or feeling in pleasant attire. At its most powerful, it is a primary means by which we link experiences both inner and outer, personal and public, past and present, actual and dreamed. Whether focused on plain reality or employed to create an imagined mind scape—whether describing the present, recounting a memory, or speculating about the future—texture is the indispensable grain and heft of a poem that hopes to be loyal toward reality.

In this anthology, certain currently popular modes of poetic cerebration and linguistic investigation are largely absent, along with some stylistic proclivities. Still, the poems in this gathering stake their vital claim on the classic themes and range considerably in tone and style. For my part, I return most often to moments of piercing descriptive clarity such as Tony Hoagland's portrait of a bedridden, dying mother in "Lucky":

> Her eyelids fluttered as I soaped and rinsed
> her belly and her chest,
> the sorry ruin of her flanks
> and the frayed gray cloud
> between her legs.

Such plain accuracy of observation carries considerable weight as the poets herein reflect on midlife. Often in these poems, the facts of bodily longing, joy, or decay are quite forthrightly confronted, as when Leslie Adrienne Miller writes in "When Hope Goes to Hug Me" of a pregnant friend, "I've been wanting / to touch the hard jar of belly." Or Kate Sontag, responding to friends and kin with breast cancer, offers in "Caribbean Breast Lullaby" a wonderfully strange secular prayer to the goddess of chance who has somehow spared her:

> Take it before it's too late to take it,
> scrubbed clean of powders, colognes, body oils,
> these last glittery grains of sand, the promiscuous
> taste of rum and sea salt, before I can no longer
>
> picture it as a rotting coconut weighing
> my lifeboat down, a woody nest of termites,
> a sack of moldy coriander seed, a milky
> jellyfish ready to sting.

Or Andrew Hudgins, in the simultaneously poignant, creepy, and hilarious "Ashes," describes cleaning up a friend's cremated ashes spilled on the floor in drunken grief:

but Johnny
        wrestled the splayed broom from my hands
and slapped the heavy ash and particles
of crushed bone toward the can.
                          "Come on now, Rachel,"
he said, "you
        wild woman you," and weeping,
Johnny stabbed and swatted at the floor
until I found a paper towel,
                wet it,
and mopped
        the last fine dust.

Poetry doesn't get much more touching (in both senses) than that. In taking the classic "dust to dust" motif quite literally, Hudgins, like many other poets here, effectively presents news that stays news.

Even when treating less tangible matters (grief, doubt, faith, love), the poems in this collection are richly embodied in a variety of ways. Cathy Song, for instance, writes of a mother's love for a newborn son with declarative directness: "My breasts were sweet for days." Jim Daniels, in "Blessing the House," a lyric of homecoming, expresses longing and regret in a more complicated but no less palpable metaphor:

Once I stood here for hours
trying to hit the streetlight with a snowball,
to leave a white smudge. I have left no smudge,
nothing I could call mine.

Leslie Ullman, in "Peace," discovers an unforgettably tactile metonym for marital tension:

Keep your voice down, my husband
hissed this morning across his plate,
then knotted his tie
to a fist that would hold
all day.

As in any honest midlife accounting, there is no shortage of anguish, doubt, disappointment, and other private or general sorrows to be found here. Perhaps that is why I am drawn so strongly to the odd moment of blessing or praise—especially when rendered with zesty specificity—the universal discovered within the particular, just as Williams advised. I love it when Thylias Moss, in "Dennis's Sky Leopard," presents a religious epiphany in imagery that would be perfectly comprehensible to the author of the Psalms:

I tilt my head, let it rain in my throat. Inside
I feel like a wheat field ready for perfect
harvest leading to ultimate feast but I'm never
cut down. That's the best part.

In a different but still celebratory vein, Bob Hicok imagines the awkward grace of his parents' mating dance in "Choosing My Conception":

So despite the shame of something
deeper showing, the unhinged self, my father
comes over between songs, lowers
my mother's head to his shoulder
and begins to sway
rigidly, like rust, until her skin
and the blue dress with one strap
almost falling, until her hands
plowing the long muscles of his back,
make him forget he hates to dance,
to douse his body in music.

Trying to explain to myself why a metaphor like "plowing the long muscles of his back" pleased me so much, I came across a passage in Jane Hirshfield's essay "The Myriad Leaves of Words." Though her topic is classical Japanese poetry, I trust the relevance to the poetry collected in *Are You Experienced?* is clear: "The trope is no decorative addition, but a fundamental tool for the seeding of meaning: by a fertile imaginative turning of outer image, we plow the ground of our lives. Japanese poetry keeps close to this primary mode of conceptualization—it uses the power held in the seen, the heard, the tasted, to quicken and instruct and unfold."

I can hardly feign objectivity in assessing this book—the editor's taste obviously overlaps largely with my own, as would be clear enough just from the poems of mine included. Still, in the best work here, I find lyrics that resonate by means of exactness of memory, honesty about complex feelings, and trust in local shades and colorings. Other anthologies will scan the immense terrain of contemporary poetry from different vantage points. This one quickens me, again and again, with the power held in the seen, the heard, and the tasted.

DAVID GRAHAM

Experience: What else is there but "experience," that is, our lives lived through the apprehension of our senses, feelings, and thoughts in the midst of events or activities leading to what we hope is wisdom, knowledge, or skill; though that isn't always a given. First, we have the witness of our senses, imbibing the details that some say God, others say the Devil, resides in. Whichever we find—whichever we set out looking for—it is in those details that poetry also resides. It's through details that the huge and crucial forces drizzle themselves down to human size: the momentary shrines and hindrances, the difficult terrain of the journey out of which wisdom is sometimes found, sometimes lost. Attention to details is a form of love, and what poetry gives is an act of imagination that allows us to see what is right in front of us, to see the ordinary in a new way. *What is* is what we most often miss.

If "the object in writing," as William Carlos Williams says, "is to reveal," that suggests the uncovering of something hidden—often from ourselves. So poetry is not a decorative art, but a kind of emotional excavation, a necessary journey. Like any pilgrimage, it's undertaken by an individual but bears fruit for a larger community. In this volume are poems that look at what we'd call ordinary experience so clearly it becomes extraordinary, as in Marie Howe's poem, "What the Living Do," in which her grief for a dead brother recasts the world with sensual immediacy:

> driving, or dropping a bag of groceries in the street,
>   the bag breaking,
>
> I've been thinking: This is what the living do. And yesterday, hurrying along those
> wobbly bricks in the Cambridge sidewalk, spilling my coffee down my
>   wrist and sleeve,
>
> I thought it again, and again later, when buying a hairbrush: This
>   is it.
> Parking. Slamming the car door shut in the cold. What you called *that*
>   *yearning.*

Other poems bend the detail toward the more figurative or surreal, as in Denise Duhamel and Maureen Seaton's childhood recollections of the cold war in "Exquisite Communist":

> Their world is red banners and small potatoes,
> soft rotten ones sprouting eyes.
> Doctors and plumbers are paid the same
> as dogwalkers. Everyone wears brown and loden green.
> Even the children blossom in shades of tan.
> The sky is a gray metal file cabinet,
> the stars full of spy secrets.

Poets at midlife: "Midway on my journey," Dante says at the beginning of the *Commedia*, and poets have been writing about that dark wood, that midpoint, ever since, using language to suggest the vividness of the lived moment, starting out like pilgrims with the specific details, not knowing where they will lead. It's a crossroads, a crux, a point of intersection at which old attitudes are reconsidered and sometimes discarded, at which new experiences act as a crucible refining or just plain burning us. W. H. Auden says poetry is "the clear expression of mixed feelings," which makes midlife a fitting context in which to explore the complexities that a few decades of living on Earth create. We're midway between youth and age, where the rising curve of energy, resolve, and recognition seems to reach an apex from which we look around. It's a point of reflection and reconsideration, high energy and frustration—an ideal time for poetry, which is triggered more by the open-ended journey that the foregone conclusion.

And so we have this gathering of poets, each one an individual, each one a part of a particular generation. Each one also is a part of a dialogue between this time and something else we could call timeless, simply because it has existed as long as we've had accounts. It could also be called tradition, history, or that larger picture that keeps appearing and disappearing in the details, as if eternity really does love time and longs to bend its unutterable self into human speech, while time returns the affection, the longing, as best it can. Think of the chills we get hearing Whitman say to us:

What is it, then, between us?
What is the count of the scores or hundreds of years between us?

Whatever it is, it avails not—distance avails, not, and place avails not.
I too lived, Brooklyn of ample hills was mine,
I too walked the streets of Manhattan island, and bathed in the waters
    around it,
I too felt the curious abrupt questions stir with in me,
In the day, among crowds of people, sometimes they came upon me,
In my walks home late at night, or as I lay in my bed . . .

Think how Sappho's sometimes plaintive, sometimes trenchant ironies still move us, the millisecond of her voice reaching across how many generations, translations, and destructions: "If you are squeamish / don't prod the / beach rubble."

As each generation bears gifts from the many that came before, each generation also makes its own way, puts the human condition into the language and rhythms of its time. We want not artifacts, but the sound of living voices, and here, in this anthology, is a record of some of those voices, poets from one specific and much observed generation, one blink of time's eye, each responding to that milli-blink of his or her own life's arc. These are poems of experience—surely we've had enough of innocence. These poems bear the fruit of complexity and irony, passions seasoned by regret. They are poems of experience in another way as well, poems selected by the editor for the way they make the individual's experience accessible to the reader, thus creating another intersection at which private and public, self and other meet, at which inner life struggles to find a shared language. These are poems selected for the way they ground themselves at those crossroads, poems in which artfulness and experience transform each other. There's Leslie Ullman's "Estrogen," in which the speaker views her life through the long end of a telescope, considering death with a remarkable sense of celebration:

> One day I too will be
> found, a lightning root
> in a sky underground,
>
> marked by whatever the years
> will have done—the fur
> my hands have stroked, the greens
>
> that pushed through soil
> and passed my lips . . .

There's Yusef Komunyakaa's taut and beautiful "My Father's Love-letters," in which the speaker negotiates the emotional complexities of his parents' separation, his father's brutality and love, with every image building toward the vivid portrait this man who

>   could only sign
> His name, but he'd look at blueprints
> & tell you how many bricks
> Formed each wall. This man
> Who stole roses & hyacinth
> For his yard, stood there
> With his eyes closed & fists balled,
> Laboring over a simple word,
> Opened like a fresh wound, almost
> Redeemed by what he tried to say.

Such a small word, *almost*, yet what freight it carries. These are poems in which the tones can be subtle, probing, complex mixtures of feeling, as in the ironic whimsy of Jane Mead's "Passing a Truck Full of Chickens at

Night on Highway Eighty," where those creatures usually considered stupid become parables of human attention and longing:

> She looked around, watched me, then
> strained to see over the car—strained
> to see what happened beyond.

> *That* is the chicken I want to be.

There are poems that explore their own possibilities, poems that use the process of composition itself as a means to break and enter new ground, as Bob Holman does in "Cement Cloud," in which the coupling of opposites and the use of nonsequiturs spark a whole new sense of what language can do. First, a reader might ask, "What?" But then come moments of recognition as we prod the rubble and find vivid fragments of our lives:

> The panic from just outside is my story holes of plane
> Flames of symbol clocks of hearts the ash and human
> And human there is first the body keep telling yourself
> That or anything because what comes next to LIFT us
> Ineffable dies in the utter unspeakability

If, on the one hand, a generation is just a blink of time's eye, on the other hand, a twenty-year span is too long to generalize about—too many variations, too many differences between those born directly after the Second World War and those born later, well into the changes their elder siblings had watched unfold or split open. Television, rock and roll, drugs, civil rights, Vietnam, birth control, feminism—we certainly saw some wild times. And we've watched fervor retreat into privacy, seen the irony of activist-turned-accountant. We've defied ourselves and seen ourselves fall. If this generation made the political personal, it also embraced the notion that the personal is political. Those two insights, along with the insistence that discrepancies between the personal and public be reckoned with, perhaps have as much to do with certain aesthetic values as the influence of confessionalism. This generation has also insisted on a greater openness to voices that were mostly left out in the past. Women and social minorities speak now, here, as never before, revealing, as Carolyn Kizer has so famously said, "the world's best-kept secret: Merely the private lives of one-half of humanity."

These days, humanity has been split into many more fractions, and you will find several of them in this anthology: the voices of women and men, people of color and different ethnic backgrounds. Tough voices like Belle Waring's "So Get Over It, Honey," and politically astute, compassionate, and outraged voices like Martín Espada, in "For the Jim Crow Mexican

Restaurant in Cambridge, Massachusetts Where My Cousin Esteban Was Forbidden to Wait Tables Because He Wears Dreadlocks." You will hear Nick Carbó's "Secret Asian Man," and Kyoko Mori's tender "To My Ancestral Spirits." For these poets, as for the generations that came before, writing is a solitary act, no matter how rich the context out of which they compose. But as this book brings them together, we can hear how the separate voices also make up a chorus for our time, imagining a future, reconfiguring the past, chronicling our compromises and losses, the painful fact of limitation: prodding the rubble until music emerges.

No anthology can say it all, and each one has its own purpose. The project of this one is not to survey all the voices and styles of contemporary poetry. The editor has assigned herself a different task, one more focused on subject and theme, one revealing another point at which voices of the inner life open themselves to the public sphere. This gathering of poems implicitly argues for poetry's ancient role in communal life, celebrating passages, exorcizing demons, invoking the divine, probing our shadows and wrestling the absurd. The voices here, for the most part, rely on colloquial speech and are given more to the subtleties of free verse than those of traditional forms. They are mostly inductive poems, drawn from the imagery and narrative of experience. They are iconoclastic, ironic, whimsical, and reflective in turn, grounded in the personal but believing fervently that the personal made vivid becomes communal. They tend to believe at least as much in language's ability to convey meaning as in its limitations. They are poems rich with surprise and attitude, each trying to bring the unutterable a little closer, poems that individually and collectively take us somewhere we would never get to without them. In the end, isn't that one thing art always does—fashion itself the vehicle for a journey that couldn't otherwise occur, moving us across centuries and continents—or just lifting our eyes so we see the world from a different angle, see ourselves in a new context? What happens next, how much poetry changes things, is up to each of us as readers.

"Midway on my journey," Dante writes, and isn't it interesting to think that he sets out with a poet as his guide, that poetry still today might be a guide?

BETSY SHOLL

I BLESS THIS HOUSE

Choosing My Conception

My mother at a party in a blue dress
dancing, left-handing a Bacardi and Coke in June
as the house pants through open windows.
Two men in the backyard clutching imaginary
nine irons, miming their swings
for the analytical reflections of the moon.
A woman seven months along in a sunflower
muumuu accepting suggestions for names—saints
and ballplayers, a candidate promising Camelot—
as hands shadow her belly, a reflex of memory.
Nancy Sinatra on the hi-fi, my mother employing
more hip, closing her eyes and shimmying
against the base line. Everyone floating
a half inch off the floor, the season
a thermal in the blood making them dream
like hawks, making them crave sky. My mother
dancing with the tide of Todd Rawlings,
with his premonitions, the air he's about
to inhabit. They don't care for each other
the way my father worries, watching
from the flagstone fireplace, Betty Thomas
composing an ode to hydrangeas in his right ear.
They don't touch each other or the lyrics,
don't know the room exists, that dishwashers
are on sale and pillbox hats a must. A little
rum, the heat of a woman finally singing
in her natural register, done
with the virginal songs, the doo-wop
tease. If for three minutes you could vanish
into your knees, into the deepest meat
of your brain, the part that thrums
hosanna, the kernel unharrowed by words,
how readily your bliss might be mistaken
for lust. So despite the shame of something
deeper showing, the unhinged self, my father
comes over between songs, lowers
my mother's head to his shoulder

and begins to sway
rigidly, like rust, until her skin
and the blue dress with one strap
almost falling, until her hands
plowing the long muscles of his back,
make him forget he hates to dance,
to douse his body in music. After an hour
of Ray Charles, Dean Martin and the diesel
of Patsy Cline, my parents leave, walk past
their red Valiant, arms vined across
each other's back, to a park where a bronze man
threatens stars with a saber. And for once
my father's able to say what doesn't
make sense but flows, to articulate
something like rhythm, she's able to forget
what he wants for a second, to look away
from his face at the willows shaking their hair
to attract the moon, suddenly they're both
devoted to the echo of a tune, the strap
of a blue dress falling, and soon,
and randomly I will exist.

I'm a Fool to Love You

Some folks will tell you the blues is a woman,
Some type of supernatural creature.
My mother would tell you, if she could,
About her life with my father,
A strange and sometimes cruel gentleman.
She would tell you about the choices
A young black woman faces.
Is falling in with some man
A deal with the devil
In blue terms, the tongue we use
When we don't want nuance
To get in the way,
When we need to talk straight.
My mother chooses my father
After choosing a man
Who was, as we sing it,
Of no account.
This man made my father look good,
That's how bad it was.
He made my father seem like an island
In the middle of a stormy sea,
He made my father look like a rock.
And is the blues the moment you realize
You exist in a stacked deck,
You look in a mirror at your young face,
The face my sister carries,
And you know it's the only leverage
You've got.
Does this create a hurt that whispers
How you going to do?
Is the blues the moment
You shrug your shoulders
And agree, a girl without money
Is nothing, dust
To be pushed around by any old breeze.
Compared to this,
My father seems, briefly,

To be a fire escape.
This is the way the blues works
Its sorry wonders,
Makes trouble look like
A feather bed,
Makes the wrong man's kisses
A healing.

To My Ancestral Spirits

They were women who spent thirty years
inside grey *kimonos*, quilting
the colors they gave up—red and pink of
childhood, green and blue of youth—into
bridal futon beddings for their
granddaughters. They outlasted the men
by decades, living on rice and a handful
of beans, toward the end growing
nothing but white chrysanthemums
for the altar.
        At forty, my mother
had a brown coat made, too old now
for her peacock blue. She asked the tailor
to line the coat with flannel, red and green
tartan no one could see. The spring of her
death, my aunt folded that coat for storage. "Your mother
still liked such bright colors," she said, brushing
the flannel with her fingers. I stored away
that remark among what I wanted to remember
most about her.
        I left my father's house
at twenty, taking only a few of her
possessions: diaries, photographs, a box of
jewelry, a sweater. My father's wife waited
to burn the rest. Out of the flames
my mother and her mothers rose up, crossed
the ocean with me. They ask me now for colors.
Through me they hunger for the yellow of
Johnny-jump-ups in the maple's shade,
the blue-purple of morning glories along white
fences. On my window sill, pink geraniums
flowered sporadically all winter, random
messages from them. Were I at my grandmother's
altar, I would offer them a red chrysanthemum,
large as my heart, a perfect globe.
Chosen by them to live in another
land, I offer my words. Their voices
name each petal, each leaf vein through me.

Blessing the House

I step out of the car and stare
at the flat houses with their bristly bushes
wild and short like my old hair.
I want to cut my hair and spread it over this snowy yard
like my own ashes, I want to curl inside a sidewalk square
my ear to the ground, cupped, listening—what could I bring
back to life? Would I hear the rough chalk scrawl over cement?

This house the priest blessed over thirty years ago
when the lawn was mud and boards. *Bless this house,*
I think, standing in the street. The wind blows cold
but I know this wind, its harsh front.
Don't try to bully me, I say. I am home
and my hands are trembling, I am sighing.
The car door slams. I clap my hands
for the hell of it, a clap on a street corner
echoing a little, among friends.

Once I stood here for hours
trying to hit the streetlight with a snowball,
to leave a white smudge. I have left no smudge,
nothing I could call mine. The grey sky presses
down on these small houses, on my parents' house
and its square slab. They are inside,
maybe changing the channel on the TV, maybe
grabbing a beer and a bowl of chips, maybe
flushing the toilet, maybe scrubbing their faces,
maybe peering out a dark window.

I am waiting to step inside for the hug and the kiss,
I am waiting to push away this grey sadness—cement and sky.
I grab a handful of snow and touch it to my forehead
where it melts down my face. I smudge my chest
with an X of snow, I toss handfuls on the yard,
on the scraped sidewalk—ashes, ashes, glowing

in the streetlight before the melting, the disappearing.
Oh glorious snow, I say, *we have missed each other.*
I listen for a moment. I lift my bags from the trunk.
The porch light glows its yellow basket
of tender light. I stomp my boots, and I go in.

How the Streets in Front of Kaufmann's Department Store Tell Me I Am Home

For years I have been lost. Some nights I have known it
        as I look out at whatever moon hung
over the wrong trees, watched as too-bright stars
        glimmered in a too-clear sky.
Other nights, sometimes for months or years I have thought
        I was home because the land

had grown familiar, because live oak and loblolly,
        palmetto or magnolia had begun to speak to me
in a tongue I understood. I said *I live here,* and the dark angels
        that flitted about my shoulders, tickling my ears
with their doubts, fell silent in front of the beauty of azaleas,
        the mystery of camellias.

But today I see that I have been gone these many years.
        Three days after snow, little rivers of cinder water
run in the gutters, ridges of plowed snow blacken
        where glass and steel cut off the sun. And
in front of Kaufmann's, in the great windows where mannequins
        show us what we *could* look like

my people—men and women wrapped in gray or brown coats,
        carrying plastic bags, lunch boxes, briefcases,
staring straight ahead or into the past—walk the crowded lunchtime
        sidewalks.
        We dodge each other, snow and ice and running water.
I'm drawn to the deli across the street, to pastrami and Iron City,
        where everyone eating big sandwiches is big

and thick, and their voices sing *Pittsburgh* when they say *Iron.*
        On the street again in the dark canyon
of Grant Street, I head for the river and Mt. Washington rising
        on its far shore. My eyes climb the tracks
on the incline, its red car inching skyward like a bucket of coal
        winched up a cliff. The Monongahela

is running high and fast, spring snow
        runoff carrying trees, beds, chairs,
and trash toward the Ohio, and I know I am home
        because from here on this bridge
I can see the Allegheny's muddy mountain water
        merge with this gray to birth the Ohio. No headwaters,

no springs rising in a quiet swamp of cattails, the Ohio
        rolls full bore past Neville Island's
abandoned steel plants, past the silence of American Bridge,
        past the gravel slab that was once Jones & Laughlin,
past my bedroom window that once saw the fire, smoke
        and ash of three shifts a day, whole valley working,

living mill lives. From here, because I know that I am home
        I can see twenty-five miles downriver as it bends
at Beaver and runs west to East Liverpool,
        where my grandfather bought his shoes and worked his first job,
and then turns south for Martin's Ferry, James Wright, and Wheeling.
        I am home today, all of us

standing in front of Kaufmann's windows, waiting
for the light to change, together at last.

Braly Street

Every summer
The asphalt softens
Giving under the edge
Of boot heels and the trucks
That caught radiators
Of butterflies.
Bottle caps and glass
Of the forties and fifties
Hold their breath
Under the black earth
Of asphalt and are silent
Like the dead whose mouths
Have eaten dirt and bermuda.
Every summer I come
To this street
Where I discovered ants bit,
Matches flare,
And pinto beans unraveled
Into plants; discovered
Aspirin will not cure a dog
Whose fur twitches.

It's sixteen years
Since our house
Was bulldozed and my father
Stunned into a coma . . .
Where it was,
An oasis of chickweed
And foxtails.
Where the almond tree stood
There are wine bottles
Whose history
Is a liver. The long caravan
Of my uncle's footprints
Has been paved
With dirt. Where my father
Cemented a pond

There is a cavern of red ants
Living on the seeds
The wind brings
And cats that come here
To die among
The browning sage.

It's sixteen years
Since bottle collectors
Shoveled around
The foundation
And the almond tree
Opened its last fruit
To the summer.
The houses are gone,
The Molinas, Morenos,
The Japanese families
Are gone, the Okies gone
Who moved out at night
Under a canopy of
Moving stars.

In '57 I sat
On the porch, salting
Slugs that came out
After the rain,
While inside my uncle
Weakened with cancer
And the blurred vision
Of his hands
Darkening to earth.
In '58 I knelt
Before my father
Whose spine was pulled loose.
Before his face still
Growing a chin of hair,
Before the procession

Of stitches behind
His neck, I knelt
And did not understand.

Braly Street is now
Tin ventilators
On the warehouses, turning
Our sweat
Toward the yellowing sky;
Acetylene welders
Beading manifolds,
Stinging the half-globes
Of retinas. When I come
To where our house was,
I come to weeds
And a sewer line tied off
Like an umbilical cord;
To the chinaberry
Not pulled down
And to its rings
My father and uncle
Would equal, if alive.

Issei Strawberry

Taste this strawberry, spin it in motion
on the whirl of your tongue, look west
towards Watsonville or some other
sleepy California town, spit
and wipe your sleeve across
your mouth, then bend down again, dipping
and rising like a piston, like fire, like a swirling
dervish, a lover ready to ravish this harvest, this
autumn of thirty-one or eight or nine, years
when, as everyone declines
around you, as swing and Capra redefine
an American dream, as some are deferred and some
preferred, and some complain, and some confer
and strike, and are stricken, are written
out of history, you have managed your own
prosperity, a smacking ripeness on the vine, acres
and acres you mine as your own, as your children's
whose deed it is, knowing you own nothing
here, you're no one here
but your genes, the ones who spit back
so readily English on their tongues, tart
and trickier, phrases that blow past
you, winking, even as they
sink in, you're losing
them, you're gaining a harvest, a country, a future,
so much to lose when, in biting your tongue,
the red juice flows between your teeth
with the memory of strawberries
and loam and sweat, of summers in the valley
when you made it before the war had come.

Habitual Offender

My oldest sister sits
eating a cracker at our dad's kitchen table.
Dad's false leg with its worn, black shoe,
lace undone, stands beside her next to the wall
by the window where gray light manages
to filter through the three-quarters shut miniblinds
stained yellow with cigarette smoke and gas fumes
from his stove's burners
which keep his little shack house way too hot. But Dad
says he'll never be warm again.
Our eyes burn and water every time we visit. Every weekend.
But, after twenty minutes or so, our eyes adjust,
and it's not so bad.
His drinking water smells.
We bring in bottled water for coffee, hide it under his sink
so we won't have to listen to him gripe
about how he's been drinking his water for going on twenty-six
    years now.
Diabetic ulcers have formed on the bottom and side
of his one foot. His toes are purple.
He suffered too much with his first amputation, he says,
to live through another one.
He's sleeping now. So we sit. My sister hands out
crackers, puts on some coffee. I'm wondering
if our brother will show up, but I'm thinking
he's holed up somewhere half-drunk, crying
in his beer, forty-five years old, waiting
for his old man to just once tell him that he loves him.

Reading Aloud to My Mother

After dinner on those last days
we hoped would linger

until the thinning moon rose
into the numb sky,

I sat beside her bed
and read from the novel she'd begun

months before on her own.
At first the words wouldn't leave

the page. Then, like crows
nibbling invisible debris

on the uneven horizon long enough
to grow invisible themselves,

they unpredictably
lifted all at once above it

and pushed across the darkening sky,
a tribe of inky letters

on a page that itself was slowly growing black
until the words, there or not, were mute

as the new moon that in a few days
would rise and fall again in the black sky

and I would be there and watching
and would not see it.

Sundowning at the Dementia Unit

Paula thanks the nurse for coming. Carter fired a nurse
yesterday after he pitched head first to the floor.
Today he says we must be ready to serve drinks
as soon as the guests arrive. Anna just counts aloud
and rocks in her chair, though yesterday
she sang a song to my dog and told him of her girlhood
in Norfolk. Kip has not yelled *God damn*! yet tonight,
but is pacing the halls as if looking for the proper time.
Jake shoves a wastebasket into the guinea pig's cage.
At dusk the whole ward is in motley motion,
even my calm, cooperative father who in mid-sentence
shuffles to the door of his room to study the hall
in both directions. "The two opposing factions
have reconciled," he reports, and I say *this is good news*.
When I ask what he saw in the corridor he looks pained
and stammers "I'm trying to get my thoughts together."
Then, as afterthought or aside, "They're getting ready
to ship the cows out of town." *About time*, I say,
as the counselor taught me. This is called *validating*.
He does not respond, but begins packing again
and asks me what time we will leave. I say
let's decide that tomorrow, and this is called *deflecting*.
I never know when he'll call me on it. Tonight,
blessedly, he just looks a little anxious and shakes
a pillow from its case, folds and refolds a shirt.

I don't know how to love this man who looks at me
vaguely as an infant, who takes my hand and lets me
lead him to the bathroom as a father will lead a son.
"What's the best way," he asks finally, "to drive there from here?"

On the Eve of My Mother's Surgery

She takes Dad, for a treat,
to the upstairs dining room,
where there are tablecloths
instead of bibs, waitresses
instead of nurses, where
all their joshing and arm-patting
make him grin like a seven
year old. But he knows where
he is, sleeping alone
for the first time in five
decades, and so he tells
Cindy in his halting
whisper all about Mom's
operation, confessing
"And I'm no help at all!"
This to a seventeen year old
with pretty face, carving
his meat into helpful cubes.

Out of the heart of dementia
he speaks unanswerable
truths, often as not confiding
in some minimum-wage
Cindy or Dawn, whose parents
weren't born when he sailed
the South Pacific in a troop ship
or cruised timber deep within
the Allagash. They will not
connect this man in diapers
with the one on horseback
in the snapshot marking his door.
At shift change they'll gun their cars
up the hill, radios screeching
and thumping, all the day's
bottled velocity released
like bees from the hive.

And it's true he's no help
anymore, stripped of his
pocketful of keys, man
without wallet or car,
who knows just enough
for honest misery
as he studies the menu's
bewilderments, trying
to find the words that may
release. "I'm walking much
better now, don't you think?"
he asks Mom, and that's true, too,
which helps neither of them
at all in their frozen love.
Sudden as a cloud across
the sun, he's overcast
again: "Keep your voice down!"
he warns her. He knows all about
the secret tunnel system
under the town, where Jews
and Mohammedans skirmish. . . .

And how do I know all this?
Out of some bent need for shape
and color, blues and riffs,
I build it from echoes
on the phone line, fragments
crumbling from envelopes,
fever dream pond ripples
reaching me a thousand miles
away. Then let my daily tears
wash into shower spray
once again, tears which
are of no help at all.

Lucky

If you are lucky in this life,
you will get to help your enemy
the way I got to help my mother
when she was weakened past the point of saying no.

Into the big enamel tub
half-filled with water
which I had made just right,
I lowered the childish skeleton
she had become.

Her eyelids fluttered as I soaped and rinsed
her belly and her chest,
the sorry ruin of her flanks
and the frayed gray cloud
between her legs.

Some nights, sitting by her bed
book open in my lap
while I listened to the air
move thickly in and out of her dark lungs,
my mind filled up with praise
as lush as music,

amazed at the symmetry and luck
that would offer me the chance to pay
my heavy debt of punishment and love
with love and punishment.

And once I held her dripping wet
in the uncomfortable air
between the wheelchair and the tub,
until she begged me like a child

to stop,
an act of cruelty which we both understood
was the ancient irresistible rejoicing
of power over weakness.

If you are lucky in this life,
you will get to raise the spoon
of pristine, frosty ice cream
to the trusting creature mouth
of your old enemy

because the tastebuds at least are not broken
because there is a bond between you
and sweet is sweet in any language.

The Moment

The way my mother bent to her car door, fumbling the keys,
    taking forever it seemed
to find the right one, line it up with the lock and feebly push it in
    and turn,
the way she opened the door so slowly, bending a bit more, easing
    herself finally into the leather seat—She'd hurt her ribs, she
    explained, but it wasn't injury
that I saw, not the temporary setback that's followed by healing,
    the body's tenacious renewal;
I saw for the first time old age, decline, the inevitable easing
    toward death. Once in the car, though,
settled behind the wheel, backing out and heading for the steady
    traffic on the highway,
she was herself again, my mother as I'd always known her: getting
    older, to be sure,
in her seventies now, but still vital, still the athlete she'd been all
    her life; jogging, golf,
tennis especially—the sport she'd excelled at, racking up
    championships—they were as natural
to her as breath. All my life she'd been the definition of grace, of a
    serenely unshakable confidence
in the body; impossible ever to imagine her helpless, frail, confined
    to walker or wheelchair.
She was humming now as she drove, that momentary fumbling
    erased, no trace of it.
No acknowledgment of pain, of the ache she must still be feeling
    in her side. My mother
refused all that, she would go on refusing it. She peered ahead at
    the busy road, the past all but forgotten—
somewhere behind us griefs, losses, terrible knowledge, but ahead
    of us a day we'd spend together,
we were going there now, while there was still time, none of it was
    going to be wasted.

My Father Calls Me Every Sunday Morning

My father calls me every Sunday morning.
Floating up out of sleep,
I can feel it coming.
He's been awake for hours.
He checks his watch,
pulls the phone onto his lap
like a recalcitrant child,
punches his Sprint code into its dumb face.
Lying in bed, I can feel each note—clear, blue as a vein—
pulsing;
through 200 miles of tense wire, my father's idea
of fatherhood speeding toward me.
And every Sunday it explodes,
precisely on schedule,
in the black box nailed to my wall.

We start with the weather: what it's doing up here,
what it's doing down there.
My father knows: everything of consequence
happens first in Baltimore, consequently
elsewhere. He instructs me on storms,
cold fronts, travel advisories, heading steadily my way.
What does he want? I've learned one trick.
I tell him a story—almost any will do—
as long as I've done or said something in it
that makes me sound like a fool.
This always works.
My father laughs.
His laugh is gorgeous.
It starts from somewhere
deep in his chest, billows up and up into the world.

When you hear it, you think of a man
striding through deep woods,
swinging his arms in the wintergreen air.
And hearing that laugh, the rise

and the rise of it,
I love him so madly. Like the tree
loves the man who comes to fell her,
her long awful groan
as she goes reeling toward earth
indistinguishable
from the lumberjack's
long roar of delight.

It's Good That Old People Get Crotchety

It's good that they complain and snap and scold.
It's good they take all day to cross the street,
glaring, holding up their hands like traffic cops.

It's good they confuse us with cousins we despised.
It's good they stink of mold and slops, and their mouths gape,
black-toothed and snoring, when they sleep.

It's lucky they fall out of bed and break their hips
at 2 A.M. and must be driven to Emergency
when we have the flu. It's fortunate they're shunted

house to house like heirloom trolls—relatives vying
to create the most convincing reasons why
they can't take the oldster, although they'd love to.

It's good each morning we're afraid to find them
dead, and hope we do. It's good they bawl—
"I'm such a burden," "After all I've done for you,"

"Nobody wants me!"—and every word is true.
It's a godsend they answer the phone,
"take" messages they don't write down,

and yell, "They've chained me to the bed!"
It's fortunate that who they were sometimes floats
above their heads, then disappears,

and it's like watching Dad devolve into The Thing.
It's good even the "Home" we finally put them in
instead of buying a car that runs, fixing our roof

that leaks—the Home that will haul us to the Poor
House in a year—can't control their tantrums any more
than we can. So it's good they curse, and shriek

like birds, and won't stop fussing with their shit.
It's fortunate the jowly minister drops by,
spends a minute with his parishioner, and an hour

proselytizing us. It's good that, at the grocery store,
we lose our appetite, passing the Depends.
It's good we've cried so much, grief has become a bore.

It's good that every atom in those ancient bodies roars,
"I need," until we scream, "Oh God, just die!"
How else could we stand to let them go?

Early Inheritance

Now I play Ben Webster with Gerry Mulligan, the album cover's a
fake fifties abstract expressionist painting, the album sleeve cracked
open like a hayseed, which I taped closed later. All of them are a bit
frayed and faded as I flip-flip-flip and find another Lester Young or
Coleman Hawkins. Some, with his name written on the side, James
Bryant—then ****! (Four Stars!) He really liked it—maybe even loved
it. It kept him company like his bottle, tuning out my mother's tirades
as everything around us crumbled. So goes another civilization—
Pompeii went in a day—so they say. My mother finally walked out my
sophomore year of college. Like Vesuvius, she blew her stack, went
through the roof and never came back. My dad was left with the
remains—and precious gems scattered in between—I mean these
records that he collected from the rubble. As one day, in a big display
of grandstanding or bluster, he brought his whole collection and hi-fi
equipment and dumped them into my room. I was fourteen at the
time. "I'm sick of your mother's bitching," he'd said, "here's your
early inheritance." He stalked out and I waited until the air was clear
and while he slept, spirited back his records and hi-fi to their rightful
place. He didn't say a word about it the next day, nor did I. I knew that
I would be probably flipping through them one day after he died—
Prez, Bird, Coltrane, Ellington. No tears now I said to myself; I must
be as cold and full of purpose as an archeologist: sort, label, and
catalogue for the archives. He would have wanted it that way. Just
a clean transfer, no glitches or worn-out clichés. Just preserve the
records I have in my possession for now, until one day when I'm too
old, I suppose, I too, will have to let them go or give them away.

Adult Child

Now that my parents are old, they love me fiercely,
and I am grateful that the long detente of my childhood
has ended; we stroll through the retirement community.
My father would like to call the woman who left me
and tell her that I will be a wealthy woman someday.
We laugh, knowing she never cared about money
but patiently taught him to use his computer and program
the car phone. In the condo, my mother navigates
a maze of jewelry, tells me the history of watches,
bracelets, rings, pearls. She says I may sell
most of it, she just wants me to know what's what.
I drive her to the bank where we sign a little card
and walk, accompanied, into the vault, gray boxes
stacked like bodies. *Here*, she says, *are the titles and deeds.*

My Father's Loveletters

On Fridays he'd open a can of Jax
After coming home from the mill,
& ask me to write a letter to my mother
Who sent postcards of desert flowers
Taller than men. He would beg,
Promising to never beat her
Again. Somehow I was happy
She had gone, & sometimes wanted
To slip in a reminder, how Mary Lou
William's "Polka Dots & Moonbeams"
Never made the swelling go down.
His carpenter's apron always bulged
With old nails, a claw hammer
Looped at his side & extension cords
Coiled around his feet.
Words rolled from under the pressure
Of my ballpoint: Love,
Baby, Honey, Please.
We sat in the quiet brutality
Of voltage meters & pipe threaders,
Lost between sentences . . .
The gleam of a five-pound wedge
On the concrete floor
Pulled a sunset
Through the doorway of his toolshed.
I wondered if she laughed
& held them over a gas burner.
My father could only sign
His name, but he'd look at blueprints
& say how many bricks
Formed each wall. This man,
Who stole roses & hyacinth
For his yard, would stand there
With eyes closed & fists balled,
Laboring over a simple word, almost
Redeemed by what he tried to say.

My Mother's Clown

Before I met your father,
she said, *I dated a clown —*
a professional clown, really, he knew
how to juggle and things, walk on his hands —
the things clowns know —
I remember
he brushed his tongue every day:
he told me he had to keep it
nice and pink,
he was always sticking it out
at children, Children want to see
a clean tongue, *he said — that was one*
of the big rules the clowns had —

Of course I imagined he was always
wearing his clown suit: my mother
arm in arm with Bozo
sashaying down the street: I must have had
the child's uncomprehending
big eyes, trying to parse it,
trying to figure out
why something would be so—

how much *better* to have married
Bozo, of course—what
a question!—what was she
thinking of, settling instead
for the serious,
the black and white, the
difficult, the gone?

My Father's Sweater

It was snug on him anyway, she said,
his wife, my stepmother, when she offered it
like a monthly magazine already read,

nothing she would miss if I took it,
something to keep me
warm in the bitter afternoon of late

March, to turn my thoughts from the empty bed
where she said he had lain for a week.
She hadn't phoned. She kept

believing he'd recover, that he'd guide her
down the hospital corridor
to their car as he'd done before,

my sleek father who'd kept slipping
into childhood, my brilliant daddy with only
saliva on his tongue.

How the worn wool glowed, how its burgundy twill
warmed me as if it were the wine
of the same name and I had had my fill.

I folded the sleeves at the wrists, pushed them up like
small accordions.
All the way home on the plane, I lay back

in my window seat surrounded
by the sad comfort of his familiar redolence.
Ten years later I'm astounded

I never wore it again. Not once have I lifted it
from the closet shelf where it lies
in the pungence of cedar, out of sight

like the soldier my father had been
in the forests of Germany, the charred
chateaux of France, where he had hidden

his fear like a stolen radio, its voices foreign
but alive, indecipherable and distant
as now his own voice has grown,

inscrutable as faith,
insistent
as the long absence of his breath.

Beneath the Canopy of Trees

—for my mother

I don't know if my mother was ever a real dancer,
but she taught dance classes; I was one of her students.

At the beginning of class we girls in our pale pink leotards
sat in a circle and imagined dipping our toes into water.

We'd arch each foot until we felt the muscles
all the way up our legs contract, then quick

curl our toes back and shriek, *Ooh, it's cold!*
Then we'd line up behind my mother with our new-found tiptoes

dotting the basement linoleum, and leap away
from the icy pool she'd had us dip them in.

Whither shall I follow, follow, follow thee?
The song we danced to was called *The Greenwood,*

and it made me feel we were underwater, submerged
but buoyant, with fathom-high trees

waving like seaweed above our heads.
My mother and I don't talk about those days,

not even when she wakes at night and needs someone
to sit her up—she doesn't have a bell to ring,

just says my name, or sometimes, *help.* Her body is heavy
in my arms, like unseasoned wood, and it's hard

to be gentle because I'm not that strong.
When her body isn't stiff it shakes: jaw, arms, hands

keeping time, each with a slightly different rhythm.
Maybe her body can't decide,

maybe part of her is still in the Greenwood. I wouldn't blame her
for wanting to go back—it's like when I forgot

my part in our recital, and was so ashamed I ran off the stage
and hid. My father said it was O.K., *we can't all be stars,*

but I think the bright lights and the sets
confused me; I wish they'd given me another chance.

My mother wants me to sit with her until she falls asleep.
The magazine she was trying to read

slides off the bed, and it seems too late, almost cruel,
to tell my mother how much I loved her

when she led us through that dark, underwater forest.
I would have followed her into anything.

II EXTENDING THE LINES

Land of the Living

Menstruation is primitive,
no getting around that fact, as
I wipe my blood from the floor
at 3 A.M. in the monastery guest room,
alone in this community
of sleeping men.

Once again, I have given up
the having of children,
and celebrate instead
a monthly flowering
of the not-to-be,
and let it go without regret.

Earlier tonight, a young monk, laughing,
splashed my face
with holy water. Then, just as unexpectedly,
he flew down a banister, and
for one millisecond
was an angel—robed,
without feet—
all irrepressible joy
and good news.

The black madonna watched us,
expectant as earth just plowed.

My sister holds her baby
in a photograph. They smile at me
from the mirror I've placed them on.
Lili sits like the Christ Child
on her mother's lap. She sits very straight
in a blood-red dress
and stares into something
that makes her look amused, and wise.

It's here, in the land of the living,
the psalm says we shall see God's goodness.
I'm glad to be here,
a useless woman,
sleepless and kept waiting,
as breath keeps coming,
as the blood flows.

Reminded of My Biological Clock—
While Looking at Georgia O'Keeffe's
Pelvis One

Pelvis with Blue, *1944*

I see so many things, a primitive ring,
a nest with a fallen-out bottom,
a white rubber band snapped into blue.
But mostly it's real memory
and the doctor holding up my X-ray
to the screen of light, a mini drive-in.
The bone was mine—big, oblong
and intact, even though my skin was purple,
my muscles sore. I'd fallen
off of Matthew's ten speed.
There were whispers that my hymen was probably gone,
first broken by the crossbar
that separates a boy's bike from a girl's,
rather than by Matthew himself. And now the X-rays
were showing my ready pelvis, an empty hammock,
just waiting for a sticky fetus sucking its thumb.
"It's beautiful," the doctor said
admiring my illuminated centerfold skeleton
before he turned to me, the real—and therefore
less interesting—thing. He smiled:
"You have the perfect hipbones, miss,
for carrying babies." To my mother he said,
"If everything else inside her is OK, someday
she'll be in labor for no more than an hour."
I was thirteen and I wanted no baby,
only a boyfriend, only some petting.
I wasn't even sure how I felt
about tongues. My favorite game was
swimming deep underwater, kicking through
a tent of spread legs, scissoring my thighs
in short quick ups and downs so I wouldn't lose
by booting someone in the crotch.
"But I don't want a baby," I might have said aloud.

My bone was a whorl in an X-ray-gray storm.
My disembodied pelvis, like a melted Hula Hoop.
"The women in our family are all Fertile Myrtles,"
my mother explained later. "When I got
pregnant with you, I think I was just
looking at your father," she said as emphatically
as if she were telling me the truth. So I found out how to get
a diaphragm and pills and foams and condoms and used them
all at once, memorizing the percentages
of their individual effectiveness: 80, 82, 89.5.
"I'm pregnant, I just know it,"
I would panic every month.
Exasperated, my first real boyfriend would remind me,
"Impossible. We didn't even have intercourse last month.
Remember? You were too nervous." In the meantime,
my girlfriends, one by one, skipped their periods.
There were trips for abortions or quick marriages.
One young mother left high school
to become a cashier at the Stop & Shop.
While she was still nursing, she leaked milk
through her shirt and smock, leaving
something like a perspiration spot
every time a baby cried in her line.
This wasn't for me, though I felt guilty,
my pelvis being the right shape and all.
My mother watched her talk shows, sometimes
on the topic of childless women, and muttered,
"How can those career ladies be so selfish?
If they don't have babies now,
they'll grow old and die alone."
Sometimes in my dreams I'm back on Matthew's bike,
not falling this time, but riding off
into the orange-cowboy sunset. Other times,
though, a crown of thorns sprouts in my belly—
my nightmare grows dark.
It is always daylight around Georgia's *Pelvises*.

The sky is the blue that the child she might have had
might have seen when he was first born.
Sometimes I dream bluebirds land on my hipbone
as though I were a round limb
on a desert tree. I feed them anything
they desire. Then the mother birds
feed their youngsters, and I tell them
they can stay as long as they like.

When Hope Goes to Hug Me

Lunged into her, my long arms stiff
from lack of this, I'm surprised how brittle,
how far gone I am. When did it end,
the ease of reaching, the circle
we mother to bring a body in? She
is distant as a film I watch,
figures from another country, fluid
in the mind, formal in the flesh. They
and she are on the other side of a glass,
a lens, a strip of tiny images, but the arm
comes in, hard and real so it frightens
all the birds in the cages of my bones.
She is pregnant, and I've been wanting
to touch the hard jar of belly,
thinking of how it would roll
under my palm, but now that she's here
clapping the old boat of me into her,
I remember the way the seed must
have found its wet mark, and the man
who launched it without full agreement.
Like me, perhaps he was shocked
by the breadth of her hug, the smell
of damp life in her hair, her toes,
all of her a place to swim, to drink,
to wash the winter's dead skin off.
She floats like her child on hope
but he's busy drawing lines
she cannot cross, lines like mine
that fall from the places on our bodies
where they're etched by days and years,
thin necklaces of flesh that we pull
from our throats and cast down to keep
the young out, to keep them from
pushing their tumescent limbs too
close. The seeds she stole from
that dry tangle of leaf and branch
were meant to die, to lie in the flake

and dust of wintry air—as my own skin,
chalky from forced air heat and dazzle
of sunlight on snow, no longer knows
how to let her near. I cook her dinner
and keep a distance, the child more
plausible in my head than in her belly.
When she leaves me I haven't touched
it as I meant to, fully, holding the whole
bulb of it in my palm. I want to, but when
her hug comes forward, her fecund breath
lifts my papery hair, my ribs rattle,
my knees lock, and I see the way I'll sleep
tonight, tomorrow and the next, the dull
book of my thighs clapped shut, my bones
folded over my heart, my womb a wrap
I've had to cast out and around me
to stay warm.

What I Did

What are you going to do
when your girlfriend's pregnant
neither of you have health
insurance or a decent job
and you've both been taking enough
drugs to kill a horse
or two?

What are you going to do
when she calls up from Wisconsin
three states away to tell you
she's pregnant, that she slipped
away the night before

she's telling you
and she's crying and she's telling you
she's going to the clinic
in the morning?

You know.
You know what you're going to do.
You're going to drive
your Plymouth Satellite all night

your head jangling
like the coins you use to call her
from rest stops to make sure
she'll wait
wait till you get there

drive all night to her sister's
in Madison and sit with her in the morning
wringing your hands and going over it
all again, slowly, and again

and you can't let yourself
think for more than a second

of the actual child
you might have together,
what you imagined while driving
when the cold air and darkness
when the lack of a radio
made all things possible

you kiss her and hold her
and wipe her nose
and wipe your nose
and you try to ignore
and not feel embarrassed by
the presence of her sister
silently circling the house.

What do you do? You drive her down
in the painful sun, the forced
squint, you pull out the wrinkled
wad of bills you conned
from friends half-gone in the bar,
you lick your fingers,
you count out your half.

What She Didn't Tell Him

A few days later, after blood
& the tearing out,
after the thumbnail embryo
had been sent on its journey
through the great waterworks
of our wastes & tender freedoms,
she remembered one afternoon
among the long days waiting
in fear, how snow fell
onto the trees, pressed
intricate lines into their
wet branches, and something,
call it joy, caught her
in happiness so pungent
she laughed, her hair glossy,
her fingers light
over the paperwork as she
thought of nothing
at all but watched snow
and felt a swift
fluttering inside her
when she least expected
lightness.

Listening

—for Samantha

And from that village, steaming with mist, riddled with rain,
from the fishermen in the bay hauling up nets of silver flecks;
from the droning of the Buddhist priest in the morning,

incense thickening his voice, a bit other-worldy, almost sickly;
from the oysters ripped from the sea bottom by half-naked women,
their skin darker than the bark in the woods, their lungs

as endless as some cave where a demon dwells
(soon their harvest will be split open by a blade, moist
meaty flesh, drenched in the smell of sea bracken, the tidal winds);

from the *torii* half way up the mountain
and the steps to the temple where the gong shimmers
with echoes of bright metallic sound;

from the waterfall streaming, hovering in the eye, and in illusion,
rising; from the cedars that have nothing to do with time;
from the small mud-cramped streets of rice shops and fish mongers;

from the pebbles on the riverbed, the aquamarine stream
floating pine-trunks, felled upstream
by men with *hachimaki* tied around their forehead

and grunts of *yoisho* I remember from my father in childhood;
from this mythical land of the empty sign and a thousand-thousand
    manners,
on the tip of this peninsula, far from Kyoto, the Shogun's palace,

in a house of *shoji* and clean cut pine, crawling onto a straw futon,
one of my ancestors laid his head as I do now on a woman's belly
and felt an imperceptible bump like the bow of a boat hitting a swell

and wondered how anything so tiny could cause such rocking
    unbroken joy.

Lucky

The baby brought us luck
from the day we brought him home.
White curtains lifted
to let in the pale lemon light.

We hung his hat on the doorknob
and raised a flag
in the shape of a fish.

The man selling corn,
the woman folding sheets,
smiled and waved their approval.
The nurse left a poem in the mailbox.

Those who visited tiptoed around
the light that had landed in our living room.
The drunk declined his usual drink.
The lady with the many bracelets
stopped her jangling in mid-gesture.
It was as if they were entering a church.

We succumbed to sleep,
the three of us and slept
through the long mornings cool
with magnolias opening beneath our window.
    His small hand curled around my thumb.
When I opened his rosebud fist, I found,
already etched, a complex map of his future.
    My breasts were sweet for days.
The smell of milk
enticed a trail of black ants
to migrate out of the Boston fern.
Like a moving signature
weaving across the carpet,
it was his first alphabet.

Abiku

—for Michael S. Weaver, Jr. 1971–1972

The only way to chase ghosts is in the tub.
I close the bathroom door and let the room
fill with steam. My mind wiggles open.
I put music on my head to seal the world
inside me and flush out infecting spirits.
I touch hurt that is twenty-three years old,
the cold potato feel of your body in the coffin
like a toy. I touch the day I went mad with
grief at your fresh grave, see the night's sky
as I rode to Crownsville State Hospital.

If I had not fathered you before marriage,
if I had not thought you would make me a man,
if I had not forgotten children's suffering,
if I had not taken this road to madness,
what road would there have been for me?
Count my gifts to you—ten months of life,
my name engraved in bronze in the earth.

When the Call Came

When the call came
I was about to cut the grass
for the first time. Wild
onion and dandelion were
sprouting across the lawn.
Sheaths of lily of the valley
bearing round green bells
were surrounding the lilac.

When the call came
the yellow marsh marigolds
were rising like the sun
against a boulder in
the flower bed. Bees
buzzed around bunches
of purple grape hyacinth.
The operator said, *I have
a collect call from Colombia.
Do you accept the charges?*
I replied, *Yes, I accept.*

When the call came
the leathery leaves
of bloodroot along the ledge
of the stone wall were
wrapped around the stalks
like green sheets on which
white petals lay. Beside
the fishpond the fronds
of maidenhair fern were
unfurling in the sun.
A voice with a Spanish
accent spoke in my ear,
*This is a social worker. We
have a baby girl born eight
days ago. Will you accept her?*

When the call came
the white blossoms
of the wild cherry at the edge
of the woods were fluttering
on black boughs. The tips
of Japanese irises were
pushing through the soil.
Specks of Bibb lettuce
lay like green confetti
on the upper level of
the rock garden. *Yes, we
accept her*, I said. *Yes.*

Geography of Love

We're living in a globe of exhaustion,
middle-aged aunts raising the orphaned boy.
Around the dinner table, we coach him
with math grids and geography facts.

We move on to his fourth-grade spelling list,
calling out words to him. By the time he packs up
his pencils and hikes off to bed, we collapse
into our weary world of tea and newspapers.

Remember how we once measured the nights?
Exploring the map of our bodies. Learning
the north, south, east and west of skin. Finger-
spelling our names, charting the way home.

Open Throat

In a child's game called dead man's float,
the winners are the most dead. It worries me
to my son's delight: how he spreads his lungs
like wings and glides over the deep end.
A web of light shadows the blue basin.

Say a soul rises when you dream it does,
and you wind up here in fear so pure
it turns into pleasure. Just like a boy
to take the worst into his waxen arms
as if it were fire. No use calling him now.

He is lost to himself, water-deaf, blind.
The charm is leaving the rope of his body.
You can see him fold into his blurred feet
then jump back through the sky's bright glass:
a child crowning into the world.

What luck! Or so we like to believe
however silly or fated it seems
later when the soft and vital parts
settle down into their dark work.
We could spend lives extending the lines

of our breath, close call after call,
delivered into one flushed affection
or another, the way a bad dream breaks
into the room it's in. We could spite
the literal heart into leaping

like a fish. My son gasps, refreshed.
It's how we come to defy gravity,
to holler backward through the open throat
at what it is that sleeps there, our bodies
pounding for admittance, swallowing air.

Falling Bricks

My daughter sings under a brick arch
of the abandoned house next door,
her stage for an audience of stones
and weeds. Her voice through glass
high and griefless, higher than it
might ever go, the sky endless
pure blue without credit cards
or betrayal.

Who can you trust? I'm making a list
of things to do—it helps me
keep control. I fold up the list
and toss it in the trash with a piece
of broken glass. When she is tired,
my daughter clutches my neck
as if it were a rope to save her.

The song has more than one name
if we have to put a name on it,
write it down—three songs
intermingled and strung together
seamlessly, like I imagine our lives
should be—mine, hers, and down
the line.

Above her, the bricks
are loosening. I should not
let her sing there, but she is perfectly
framed like a saint in an altar.
I hold my own neck like that,
to imagine the comfort she takes.
My skin is loosening there.
Oh, my beautiful child,
do not trust me.

Teasing Was Only the Beginning

In this picture my son's face
is young, dark circles I never saw before now
under his eyes, his face turned a bit,
his mouth open as if he's inhaling or saying
ahhh, but overall his expression is happy.
His expression at the dinner table
was happy, his hair yellow
as the hay he'd helped my husband mow.
Dishes and silverware clattered; in those days
I cooked meat and corn, gravy and bread—
food for growing children and a hard working man.
My husband was a hard working man,
his face washed just before he sat down, his hair
wet and combed straight back, the illusion
of order, a clean smell.
His cheeks shone and he tapped the table
with his fork, threw a comment to my son,
just a small crack, what my mother called
teasing.

Teasing was only the beginning.
My son's face crumpled—that's the only word for it—
and began to split and split again
as if he were something divided by a knife,
barn dust streaking his face.

The barn dust on his face
ran in rivers into this mouth, and, I think,
his world must have dissolved,
compressed into a small, hard welt in his lungs,
the labor of breathing, trying to mingle
corn and saliva, trying to hold back.
I held back, believing a second marriage
might only be saved if parents stood together
in matters of the children, since the children
were another man's—really only mine.

I took a deep breath and concentrated
on a blue spot or a gold kernel of corn,
anywhere but on the contorted face
of this boy who sat, head up, eyes on the man,
fork poised over the meat.

From the Temple of Longing

The moment the children climb
into my ex-wife's car they buckle
themselves into a faraway look.
The little one
never cries, the eldest
counts white hairs that sneak
like the future up the side of his arm.
Camel, tent, oasis, storm—their ancestors
longed to pause and longed even more
to press on. But on a cobalt dark
night like this, following
an invisible need at the other
end of a leash, I want to hear
from my wild nomads dreaming
on the other side of the state. I want
to hear them say papa, it's alright,
don't cry—always thirsty at three a.m.
for something more than water. Maybe
you think this is all about a dime-
a-dozen emotional flotsam who left a furious
marriage only to miss his children from one
school holiday to the next, who exaggerates
the tangled heartworms that pressed
his ribcage when his
parents divorced. Maybe you just
want to tell me that children
are not that fragile. But I wonder
what I would hear, a dozen
years from now, waiting for the last
solar eclipse of the century, my arms relaxed
around my teenage boys, hovering
over a jerryrigged
cardboard theater, watching
the little moon erase the little sun—
I wonder what they would say
in that strange light, if I asked them
to remember.

Children of Divorce

"We should imagine that we are in heaven,"
I read, as the pilot announces a holding pattern.
Two children of divorce
are busy with the game of "Doorbell."
"Who's there?" they scream
every time
a bell sounds; they pretend to look for faces
in the storm clouds.
The stewardess has seated them together,
a boy and a girl,

pretending not to be afraid.
"We should imagine that we are in heaven,"
insists Theodore of Mopsuestia, a name
the children would adore, no doubt
a close relation of Mopsy
Cottontail. The world robes itself
in ribbons of light, each inundated place on earth
a shiny coin, a medium of exchange
in the brooding dark through which we pass.
The girl asks, "Can a tornado pick up a plane and throw it?"
The boy says, "I can't look, it's too scary,"

as he pulls down the window shade.
"It's an ocean down there,"
says the girl, "we'll be lost at sea."
"It's too scary," the boy says again,
lifting the shade
as the pilot announces our approach for landing
in Minneapolis. Theodore
and the girl are right:
it doesn't look like any world we know.

"We're gonna die," says the girl,
"I can't look," says the boy, "we're not gonna make it."
"Oh, is that the city—aren't the lights pretty?"

"We're not gonna make it."
The great river shines in the newly minted dusk—pale
and black; red, white—"He'll never make the runway,"
says the boy, "we're gonna die." "Oh," says the girl,
"just look at the lights."

Family Reunion

The divorced mother and her divorcing
daughter. The about-to-be ex-son-in-law
and the ex-husband's adopted son.
The divorcing daughter's child, who is

the step-nephew of the ex-husband's
adopted son. Everyone cordial:
the ex-husband's second wife
friendly to the first wife, warm

to the divorcing daughter's child's
great-grandmother, who was herself
long ago divorced. Everyone
grown used to the idea of divorce.

Almost everyone has separated
from the landscape of a childhood.
Collections of people in cities
are divorced from clean air and stars.

Toddlers in day care are parted
from working parents, schoolchildren
from the assumption of unbloodied
daylong safety. Old people die apart

from all they've gathered over time,
and in strange beds. Adults
grow estranged from a God
evidently divorced from History;

most are cut off from their own
histories, each of which waits
like a child left at day care.
What if you turned back for a moment

and put your arms around yours?
Yes, you might be late for work;
no, your history doesn't smell sweet
like a toddler's head. But look

at those small round wrists,
that short-legged, comical walk.
Caress your history—who else will?
Promise to come back later.

Pay attention when it asks you
simple questions: Where are we going?
Is it scary? What happened? Can
I have more now? Who is that?

Making Step Beautiful in Maine

*[Nature] seems to say sternly, why came ye here before your time? . . . Is it not
enough that I smile in the valleys? . . . Why seek me where I have not called thee,
and then complain because you find me but a stepmother?*
—*Henry David Thoreau,* The Maine Woods *(1864), speaking of Mt. Katahdin*

Someone has to do it:
        extract
                the mackerel bone
                the gooseberry spine
                the rose hip seed . . .
                        from our throats.

    And what better place than these woods rising out of
Penobscot Bay where my husband's daughters who've summered
    here since birth teach me how to identify from within
this edible golden carpet of chanterelles
    the poisonous look-alike jack-o'-lantern
with the *true* gills.

        The origin of Step may be as one of them suggests
                a parent one step removed from blood
                  or as the other offers
        a parent who steps in to help like a stepladder

but for most of us the word has always

        fallen like rotten summer apples
            that linger and ferment in our backyards
            intoxicating the yellow-jackets

        bitten us like horseflies and blackflies
            at the granite quarries
            then smelled up the car like a wet dog

        buzzed in our lamplit hair like Junebugs
            on the deck after a dinner of
            mussels gritty with pearls

loomed like the Milky Way's invisible black hole
over midnight harbors
as mosquitoes send us inside.

Today stepsails float magically on the horizon
a stepmoon offers translucence in the late afternoon in sky
stepgrass holds our footprints in fading light
each stepshadow crosses the other
as stepbirds sing us into this starry stepnight
sweet note by sweet stepnote home.

Father of the Man

Your daughter, fifteen, has drunk a half bottle
of gin, passing out in the bushes.
Her boyfriend's car costs twice what your first house did.
Blood of your blood, heart root blossoming,
still she does not figure in this story.

For a more bitter car now squeals away.
The hair you've lost is not entirely gone:
see, it returns on your son's clenched jaw
as he plays air guitar in his bedroom,
his walls all Nazi regalia, his dreams
all wind-stunned and far from this sick village.
Yes, here is the hard seed you recognize.

No, he won't go to the ballpark with you.
He's tired of your beery friends, your tapedeck
spewing sixties junk, throbbing blue vein
rising on your temple. And old? He's never
seen such a decrepit father, when you've
tipped a few and begun leering at
the available wives, sometimes even
stripping your shirt off for volleyball. . . .

And you know that *grump grump* bass that rises
all evening from his basement hideout?
It's nothing but your sullen, well-mapped fate.
It's all those wind-in-the-blood whiskey nights
you vowed never to forget or regret.
It's dust spraying as you popped your wheelies
through the vacant lot that's now a realtor's.

It's the open legs of your dream at last
beckoning—no, you can't leave her out now—
her prom-night giggle and hushed, skinnydipping
waters you still feel throb in your belly.

Bass and drum, the synthesized wail rising
to the night trees—father, it's all you ever
hoped or could be, this welcome capsizing
and perfect acquittal. This shutout game
you'd never have trusted when you were your age.

Chances

Behind the car peeling out with my daughter,
the boy's a cartoon of running, arms pumping,
legs high. I can't help thinking *thief*, like the kid
I saw in New York once, coming out of a store,
clutching something under his coat. *Hey,*

my friend called, *drop it*, and he did—boom box
splitting apart on the sidewalk as he took off.
Now the car rounds the corner again, honks
to make this boy look up from his gasping
and climb in. *Hey, Baby*, my daughter calls,

half her body stuck out the window—
sixteen, off for a night at the boardwalk,
where everyone's part cheat, trying to con
the numbers and iffy rides, toss darts
against the odds neon flashes through slats

onto the dark water brooding below.
The tide's contained now, but come a storm,
it'll swell and batter the pilings, tumble a girl
like dice on a wheel. I have flashbacks—
waves heavy with sand, crashing down so I can't

get my head out. You'd think I dropped as far
as Pip, the cabin boy in *Moby Dick*,
plummeting though briny sub-basements
where the world's weight is stored, tumbling,
bottomless, nothing to stand on. What could he do

after that, but stare, bug-eyed, addressing himself
in third person like the people on park benches
ducking mortar from an old war, or nodding
to a conversation started years ago?
On the pier where the kids wander from ride

to ride, my daughter will turn the barkers' heads
with her yellow hair, as she goes to test
night's loud music and chintzy lights, shrieks
scattered over the water from frenzied carousels.
Easy enough to shrug, *Why not*—this edge,

huge ocean rolling in, against which
we pitch our ridiculous coins. Why not
plunge through the mazes and wheels
of those rigged games, taking another
and another chance, trying for some

perfect shot to realign our lives?
But that's not how it felt the night my child's
blood pressure dropped, and her life flickered
so far from jackpot she didn't want to wake up.
Too late for a stomach pump, they ran IVs

and I don't ever want to see again
that shade of pale and fear. Later, she flushed
what was left of those pills. We held each other
watching them swirl, and if I can say this now,
it's because sometimes the waves spit us back up—

Delivered from the deep, Jonah says.
And that's how the houses look near the boardwalk
on their green weedy stilts, one with a wall
like the slat backing of an old radio
showing the circuitry inside, wires and tubes

where current flows. Does every kid half-live
in the radio, receiver tuned to those jacked-up
voices of longing and rage? I can still hear
Cousin Brucey advertising Palisades
Amusement Park, its tattooed barkers

with their nicotine kisses calling *Baby*,
Baby, as if we went there to lose our names,
whispering, *any life but mine.* Poor Pip.
The harpooners stood up to aim, and without
thinking he jumped, then found to his surprise

there isn't another life. Refuse our own,
and we're left to drift between stations,
on oceans of static. Imagine—the boats
take off, the huge water expands its bad trip
around you. Terror in the depth, terror

in the width. *Heartless immensity, my God!*
Melville writes—as if vastness dissolves us.
To keep himself solid, Jonah quoted psalms
in the belly. When the dark rose up like waves
slamming my daughter, she says she drifted

in and out, repeating all night, *don't die.*
It takes my breath away—to think how the pills
we saw spin down the drain could have swallowed
that voice, swept it out so far she'd never get back.
It's happened enough. You can see them

on the boardwalk, drifters caught in the undertow.
They mutter to figments of themselves, ask
for spare change or a light, hoping to strike up
with a girl young enough to misread the signs,
and I can't help being relieved when my daughter

comes in, telling how a barker slowed down
the wheel so she could bring home this glass vase,
the color of water, air bubbles trapped inside
like breath rising from a diver, its value
in all the chances she took to get it.

Fatherhood

Your life will be half-over when you arrive
at this porch yourself, the stars close and clear
through your breath, the moist, misted breath
of the one world we all contribute to, fully present,
quivering with distances. And if the back-light
from your kitchen door throws a skewed rectangle
into which you fit like a coffin,
know that I'm behind you then, helping you
not to turn around, helping you to stand straight up,
taking in the blades of cold, going on and on,
though your body stays rooted firmly
at the edge of all you've built.

Once my dirt is turned, your gardening begins,
and so I offer this soil I didn't know I was making,
this darkness from which flower light arcs,
perennial, inextinguishable,
spearing all with beauty.

Drive the trowel deep, separate the ribs,
tamp far into me your guilt and shame. I will
no longer be separate from you then, together
as we could not be while I lived. We'll be as lilies
sprouted from the same bed, having gouged out our place,
now bowed with rain, now upturned and listening.

And I will be with you on your father's rounds,
this late, when the only sound is your neighbor's heat pump,
and the hanging plants twisting on their chains,
once you have been compelled back into the house,
floorboards shifting beneath the carpet.

The nightlight in the children's bathroom
glows on the bath toys in the hall.
Nothing has been put back,
which means all is where it ought to be, and
the children, exhausted after a long day

of touching everything they own at least twice,
seem to have fallen from jungle gyms
into their beds, their lips dry when you kiss them,
their faces cool, their hearts rhythmic in some dream place.

From one room to another in the house of yourself,
surprising a silverfish, straightening frames,
repositioning your mother's pillows on the olive couch;
that's how I see you, turned inward, finally,
having acquired something to lose,
a shadow in boxer shorts bending over the sleepers
with the weight of fatherhood
like a sleeping newborn on your chest,
her ear to your heart.

Soon you will turn even deeper into the house
and the warmth of a woman who will forgive your absence
if only you turn fully and to her alone.

Just a little while longer, you'll think,
then I'll go to bed,
just one more moment
and perhaps they'll smell your skin, sense you there,
perhaps dream of you watching over them,
doing what you can to accept the darkness for what it is,
to leave it outside pressed against the windows,
leaning in its turn, over all of you.

Those Things

Preparing to talk to my son, I remember
my father in the hospital bed, slowly
becoming tangled and lost among a maze
of tubes, and when from a chair by

the window I asked if there was anything
he regretted, he answered, "I'd go to
church and I'd have talked to you about
those things." With long strokes

that bent my body like an oarsman,
I massaged his swollen calves.
We had never touched except
to shake hands, and only once

did I cry to his face, when I accused
him of not caring, when I was
young and cared, but in those last
months, when flowers lined

the window sills and I read
to him, we held hands. I never
saw him naked, and I haven't
seen my son naked in years,

though I know his body is being
driven to collide with others.
Yesterday on the basketball court,
when he raised his arms to shoot,

I saw dark tangles of hair.
I wonder what more it was
my father had wanted to tell me
that one evening just after I had

learned to drive, and he walked
over to the Volkswagen. I started
the engine, and he leaned toward
the window, as if to whisper.

Though no one was near, his hand
covered the side mirror when he said,
"Protect yourself." That was it
and I backed out of the driveway.

Comfort

We have everything we need to believe right here in front of us.
— Dabney Stuart

I put my mouth on the wound of the tree.
I breathed, a child in my father's yard.
My breath was a Valentine, came from my red heart.

The tree lived long past the time of its wound.
My father went to his grave, and I believed in his death.
In the yard I would do his work, taught my children his name.

My mother inside the window watched us
and we turned to wave, her love for us involuntary,
streaming through the glass; she held her position.

My oldest son said, high in the branches of the tree,
"Here are his arms, I am swinging from his arms."
The tree turned to me, promised to live until I could do

without him.

III

WOVEN IN MY WALK

Willing

He says you're a blackberry, dropped into his mouth
by a crow, says *Sweet, sweet girl* to the damp of your neck.
It's afternoon. Through your squint, foxtail splinters,
blonde as the half-slip we fight over in the catalogue,
the demi-cup bra, satin-strapped and less candid
than this boy's hands. He'd wear you like skin if you'd let him.

He says locusts told him where to find you,
that your blue dress is plenty deep for two;
and you're starting to trust the muscle
all this wanting gives you. Your shoulders come back
when a car full of boys rockets by on the two-lane, pulling dust
and a long howl. All the way out to the interstate,
they talk about turning around.

Now your arm is beside you, bent, like a page you'll return to.
He says *Listen*, then stops talking. What comes next isn't news:
his sudden flush and bloom. Then the cell-like splitting
of this day into two, four, eight identical others.

I pass the shape you've tamped into the grass.
It looks like an animal has circled before sleeping. I lie down,
willing anything: a ripple, rain. I lick my hand.
There is no tinge of blackberry, no hint of what's coming.

Freight

Now I see that the first boy I loved
loved speed for its own sake the way
we all loved our bodies before learning
to feel ashamed. He built plywood ramps
on parking lots all over town and crouched
on a skateboard as it swooped and shot
across asphalt. His orange VW careened
down steep mountain roads the one night
we sneaked off and drove almost to dawn.
Yet he could be patient, sweet,
unable to believe I'd never been kissed
at fifteen, though I earnestly practiced
tilting my head back, fluttering eyelids,
tonguing the end of my fist so I'd know
what to do when he took me in his arms
in the dark in the woods when I would not
refuse what I knew must be the drive
that can wreck a girl, despite her own
intentions. That whole brutal summer
I pulled weeds in my father's garden,
my body stunned by its great momentum
and a halting restraint like bad brakes.
Once I stood up light-headed in the sun
certain I'd drop over dead with desire,
dense and pure as lead in my veins,
but I never succumbed, and in the end
we both accused the other of loving less.
For the next decade I plodded through school
and married while he dropped out, drove
customized vans to dealers throughout
the Midwest, then moved east, delivering
papers too precious to fax. Last I heard,
he works for the railroad running freight
through Pennsylvania at night when tracks

are clear of passenger trains. Sometimes
I wake to a distant whistle and think
of his engine somewhere in the mountains
rushing toward Baltimore or Williamsport,
nothing to stop him.

Providence

I walked away with your face
stolen from a crowded room,
& the sting of requited memory
lived beneath my skin. A name
raw on my tongue, in my brain, a glimpse
nestled years later like a red bird
among wet leaves on a dull day.

A face. The tilt of a head. Dark
lipstick. *Aletheia.* The unknown
marked on a shoulder, night
weather in our heads.
I pushed out of this half-stunned
yes, begging light, beyond the caul's
shadow, dangling the lifeline of Oh.

I took seven roads to get here
& almost died three times.
How many near misses before
new days slouched into the left corner
pocket, before the hanging fruit
made me kneel? I crossed
five times in the blood to see

the plots against the future—
descendent of a house that knows
all my strong & weak points.
No bounty of love apples glistened
with sweat, a pear-shaped lute
plucked in the valley of the tuber rose
& Madonna lily. Your name untied

every knot in my body, a honey-eating
animal reflected in shop windows
& twinned against this underworld.
Out of tide-lull & upwash
a perfect hunger slipped in

tooled by an eye, & this morning
makes us the oldest song in any god's throat.

We had gone back walking
on our hands. Opened by a kiss,
by fingertips on the Abyssinian
stem & nape, we bloomed
from underneath stone. Moon-pulled
fish skirted the gangplank,
a dung-scented ark of gopherwood.

Now, you are on my skin, in my mouth
& hair as if you were always
woven in my walk, a rib
unearthed like a necklace of sand dollars
out of black hush. You are a call
& response going back to the first
praise-lament, the old wish

made flesh. The two of us
a third voice, an incantation
sweet-talked & grunted out of The Hawk's
midnight horn. I have you inside
a hard question, & it won't let go,
hooked through the gills & strung up
to the western horizon. We are one,

burning with belief till the thing
inside the cage whimpers
& everything crazes out to a flash
of silver. Begged into the fat juice
of promises, our embrace is a naked
wing lifting us into premonition
worked down to a sigh & plea.

Ang Tunay Na Lalaki Moves into Sally's Apartment

on 5th Street between Avenues B and C.
His plaid boxer shorts are already neatly tucked
in the bedroom drawers, shirts hanging
in the walk-in closet, most of his books on her shelves,
lap-top in a corner of the living room, and his toothbrush
and shaving supplies sharing her medicine cabinet.

There are three large railroad-type rooms
which can accommodate two sofas each, lots of wall space
for his posters of the Banaue rice terraces,
the chocolate hills of Bohol, the Mayon Volcano,
the sailing Vintas of Zamboanga, and of the old walled city
of Intramuros, Manila. The kitchen has a 50's dinette set
with a formica top, a full-range oven which had already been
baptized with the pungent spills of his Filipino cooking.

It was after he had cooked his sixth dinner
for Sally when he slipped the diamond engagement ring
into her halo-halo (a dessert with shaved ice, filled
with tropical fruit, sweet cassava, and milk and sugar).
"I hope you haven't made this special halo-halo
for every woman you've met," she said, slipping
the ring on her finger. "It fits! When can you move in?"

When I Was Straight

When I was straight I dreamed of nipples,
my dreams were crowded with cleavage and yin,
I read a book that said if you are fickle

about sex, note your obsession in dreams
then do the opposite in real life. This
made sense, my boyfriend said, although it seemed

oddly like a game of Exquisite Corpse
to me. We'd make love, I'd dream of figs,
that drizzled pink, and sometimes I'd lapse

into madrigals (meaning: of the womb), big
leap from the straightforward sessions in bed
of linearity and menthol. Legs

would cross and uncross in my dreams, heads
fall back with me at the throat. I adored
the winged clavicle, that link between breast-

bone and scapula. Straight as gin, I poured
myself into pretense and fellatio,
you could count on me for bold orgasms, for

trapeze art and graceful aerobics, oh
there is no lover like a panicked lover.
Once I dreamed of abandoning the Old

Boyfriend Theory of Headache and Blunder-
buss. Believe me, I said, this will hurt him
more than me, but the dream laughed! Torture

me, I thought, now that even my id
has turned against me, there is something fragile
here to lose, exquisite truth, and I did.

Two Men on a Swing Watching
Their Shadows Lengthen

Pruned back last winter, the grapevines
start to bud mid-May, the arbor still
too white with a new coat of paint.
Another robin crashes into the earth,
its carcass scattered by the blades
of a reconditioned mower. The swing
slows. You touch my knee, and I hear
the brass weights of a grandfather clock
steadily falling in that cottage where
we met, the season's first snow fresh
on the ground as hands ran up and down
a polished cherry cabinet built
to last. Like barrels of oak fermenting
in the dark. Is life nothing more
than two men on a swing watching
their shadows lengthen? No more music
stirs in that room, only a window
overlooking a yard with a birdbath
filling up with snow. Touch me again
even while an ant on a rotten stump
struggles to carry a petal underground.

Wedding Party

I wanted to have a wedding
where a band called Sexual Chocolate
would play cover versions
of "Turn the Beat Around"
and "Got to Be Real," tunes
so disco everyone's forsaken them
in the oh-so-cynical '90's.
I wanted my bridesmaids
in orange tulle, groomsmen
in light green, their cummerbunds
so wide their waists became
some thick, enticing region,
regal as an alleyway.
I wanted folks to glide
onto the dance floor,
doing quaint, antiquated dances
like the funky chicken, Latin hustle,
polyester divas doing moves so fine
even Shaft himself would have
to stop, grin his approval.
I wanted finger foods
in snack sizes, a wedding cake
piled so high in gumdrops
and coconut that no one's
blood sugar level would be safe.
I wanted it crass, and big,
and ugly, bad enough
to make relatives shudder
whenever they remembered
my denim patchwork gown,
platform heels. Instead,
I'm here at the city clerk's office,
an ordinary woman in an
ordinary dress, marrying
an ordinary man in ordinary
shoes. Still, I know that party
is going on somewhere, if only

in the strange regions of my mind:
music and costumes
by Earth, Wind, and Fire,
catering by Momma and Company,
and the m.c., of course,
is a dapper black man
who wishes us *love, peace, and soul,*
our lives one everlasting ride
on the Soul Train bound
for Boogie Wonderland,
li'l Stevie's harmonica
blowin' us one last tune
in the key of life.

Marriage

Long ago I came through the prairie,
mountains broke from the earth and rose
up. I was afraid and said the prairie was
finished.

I do not follow the blood blue line
on the map that would lead me to the San Juan mountains.
I assume they do not exist, have little to teach me.
I drive in a circle, a complicated and beautiful circle,
and prairie, prairie, prairie is my choice, is all I see.

Making Love

Why *make*? I used to wonder.
Is it something you have to keep on
making, like beds or dinner, stir it up

or smooth it down? Sex I understood,
an easy creaking on the upholstered
springs of a man you meet in passing.

You *have* sex, you don't have to make it,
it makes *you*—rise and fall and rise again,
each time, each man, new. But love?

It could be the name of a faraway
city, end of a tired journey you take
with some husband, your bodies chugging

their way up the mountain, glimpsing
the city lights and thinking, *If we can
keep it up, we'll make Love by morning.*

I guess it was fun for somebody,
my grandmother once said. By then
I was safely married and had earned

the right to ask, there in the kitchen
beside the nodding aunts. Her answer
made me sad. In her time, love meant making

babies, and if I had borne twelve
and buried three, I might see my husband
as a gun shooting off inside me, each bullet

another year gone. But sex wasn't my question.
Love was the ghost whose shape kept
shifting. For us, it did not mean babies,

those plump incarnations the minister
had promised—flesh of our flesh,
our *increase*. Without them, and twenty years

gone, what have we to show
for the planing and hammering, bone
against bone, chisel and wedge,

the tedious sanding of night
into morning, when we rise, stretch,
shake out the years, lean back,

and see what we've made: no ghost,
it's a house. Sunlight through the window
glazing our faces, patina of dust

on our arms. At every axis, mortise
and tenon couple and hold. Doors
swing heavy on their hinges.

After Making Love, We Hear Sirens

. . . Two women sleeping
together have more than their sleep to defend.
—Adrienne Rich

Here in the center of town—one block
from the fire station, two blocks from the hospital,
four blocks from city hall, where I work
in a steel and bulletproof glass-encased police station—
we hear sirens all the time. Yet, for some reason,
they seem most likely to sound—not while we are cleaning,
eating supper, playing with the dog, reading quietly
at opposite ends of the couch—but at moments like these,
as we lie side by side, naked, whispering,
singing stupid old songs to each other.
Light from the hallway spills into the room,
glints on the badge I've left atop the dresser
in the dust neither of us has time to wipe off.
I remember the first time I pinned that badge
to my uniform shirt, carefully centered my name tag
over the right chest pocket, went off to keep the city safe.
It was what I'd wanted forever, until I wanted you.
In another city, another state, loving you might be a crime—
and then what badge could I wear, what justice for us,
what sirens would we listen for?

Looking at Your Body

—for Renée

As you walk
to the mirror
and drop the towel
to the floor,
the beads of water
still pock
your smooth white skin.
You look with disapproval—
almost chagrined.
You pat the womb-worn tummy,
the too-solid
widening of the flanks.
Suddenly,
the gentle dips and bends
of country culverts,
deep ditches filling
with spring rain
appear as your body
simply has shifted a little in time,
grown over in places
or filled in somewhere else.
Yet, standing before you
I look at your body
for the first time as
in that field of ripe October corn
west of your parents' house.
Dusk, stretched out
naked as a jaybird,
we followed the rows
ear to ear
into the darkening west,
two limbs of a
windblown poplar
bent down
to finally embrace.

Milk

Given your birth, I am the glue of the cosmos. Love, I am
what wakes you, puts you to sleep, keeps you going.
I am fluid matter, essential as swallows
of air.

Out of love for you I spew a breezy spray from a zillion flesh-cracks.
I made the thick white path across the night.
I made the pillow smell of you.
I made your muscles and dreams thicken with meaning.

Do you know I created a world out of a chapped nipple?
Do you know I made the hills round (you thought it was wind
    and erosion).
I even made the neck bone
of the moon.

So charged is my love, when I hear you cry I surge toward you
like an electrical current. When you are brought near me
I tingle and pulse. Even the curdled smell of me
in your sleepy mouth makes me rise up. Tongue to teat,
this is my love for you.

I am ordained as the stickiness between you and your mother.
That cellular blur, that cave of sleeping eggs, sperm sacs, the elixir
when you focus and find the eyes,
the sudden union.

When you sniff me out with eyes shut, wiggle fingers and toes,
wag your head, latch on like a pup and suck, I come
oozing out of both breasts, out of all the udders, teats,
cracks, and you slurp and squeal like a pig in paradise:
this is my pleasure and purpose.

I will dry up and seem not to matter only when you turn away
with the teeth I made for you, with your hunger
for other things. You may think I am full
of myself, but you are wrong.
It is you who is full of me. I am nothing
without you. I am your marrow.

Never forget me.

What Difference Does It Make?

When the giant panda views another
of her species through a window, in a mirror,
does she feel a little less lonely?
I smile when I see another couple like us,
though of course they aren't like us,
except for the contrast
between white skin and black.

The year I turned twelve
the way we live was still a crime;
then *Loving v. Virginia* made race irrelevant
in marriage, told Richard and Mildred they could live
where they were born.

I thought it nothing to write about,
only one kind of difference in a world of difference,
no shame and nothing to brandish like a badge.
I thought that what should not matter, did not.

Other see an *odd couple,*
all she could get, a trophy, a burden.
Has he bought my whiteness with his maleness?
Or does his blackness accompany my womanhood
in the same swampy place?

Through his eyes I see the pain
of interviews that go well on the phone,
the equivocal compliments, followed by *for a . . .*
But I can choose not to see it at all,
as my white skin carries me like a sail.

If you flayed us, you'd notice only the sex,
but it's impossible to live without skin.

Whenever I blurt the word "racist,"
I want to retrieve it, as when
I called a child, "illegitimate";
that night my husband asked,
"What difference does it make?"

Epithets are helicopters
with swords for blades,
but also methods of transport
from here to there.

What our families didn't say and do
was not kind, and then we grew through it like a tree
whose roots invade sewer lines.
Good things—eating, learning, love—
demand openings, penetration,
marriage.
To let the other in,
to not say, *not us*.

Wild Strawberries

In this weedy field somewhere inside marriage,
snuggled under thistles and nettles, we find them,
bright promises. Down on our knees like penitents
or children, we pick, our tongues puckered and bloodied,
our careless hands stung red, the sun plumping
ripe and peppery in the July sky.

This morning we fought over nothing
I can remember, pride springing up all around us,
with its barbs and hooks. Now all afternoon
I've been thinking how we'll grow old together,
our perennial violence and tenderness,
bearing less and less.

Back in the city, the markets stock strawberries
bred for safe shipment, long storage,
crisp and predictable in their stacked flats.
Here, as we carry our berries back to the cabin,
back to our dangerous lives,
we know they are so fragile and ripe

their own weight in the bowl could ruin or bruise them
beyond texture, or beauty, or definition.

The Couple

They no longer sleep quite as well as they did when they were
younger. He lies awake thinking of something that happened a long
time ago, turning uncomfortably from time to time, pulling on the
blankets. She worries about money. First one and then the other is
awake during the night, in shifts, as if keeping watch, though they
can't see very much in the dark and it's quiet. They are sentries at
some outpost, an abandoned fort somewhere in the middle of the
great plains where only the wind is a regular visitor. Each stands
guard in the wilderness of an imagined life in which the other sleeps
untroubled.

After Fighting for Hours

When all else fails,
we fall to making love,
our bodies like the pioneers
in rough covered wagons
whose oxen strained to cross the Rockies
until their hearts gave out trying,
those pioneers who had out-survived
fever, hunger, a run of broken luck,
those able-bodied men and women
who simply unlocked the animals
from their yokes, and taking
the hitches in their own hands, pulled
by the sheer desire of their bodies
their earthly goods over the divide.

Near Heron Lake

During the night, horses passed close
to our parked van. Inside I woke cold
under the sleeping bag, hearing their heavy sway,
the gravel harsh under their hooves as they moved off
down the bank to the river. You slept on,
though maybe in your dream you felt them enter
our life just long enough to cause that slight
stirring, a small spasm in your limbs and then
a sigh so quiet, so close to being nothing
but the next breath, I could believe you never guessed
how those huge animals broke out of the dark and came
toward us. Or how afraid I was before I understood
what they were—only horses, not anything
that would hurt us. The next morning
I watched you at the edge of the river
washing your face, your bare chest beaded with bright water,
and knew how much we needed this,
the day ahead with its calm lake
we would swim in, naked, able to touch again.
You were so beautiful. And I thought
the marriage might never end.

The Bull's Eye Inn

Apologies to T. S. Eliot for the first two lines.

Let us go then,
you and I,
to the Bull's Eye Inn,
through the rusted iron gates
into the dark and damp, stepping on saw-dusted
floors gushing with ether, where my ex-wife
once waited tables on weekends grinning with death.
Come to where the blood, beer, and barf
flowed with the bourbon washes.

My ex-wife often invited me to watch over her.
My job on those weekends, she explained,
was to sit in a dark corner, by myself,
and keep the out-of-work mechanics,
the foundrymen
and slow-talking *cholos*
from going too far—
which was like blowing a balloon
and trying to stop just before it burst!

Dudes would buy her drinks
and she brought the drinks over to me.
Laid back against a plush seat,
I silently toasted
their generosity.

I did a toast to her too, to our babies,
to the blood-shot eyes of East LA nights
and the midnight romps we once had,
near naked, in the park.

Many times in the candle-lit haze,
as a disc jockey played tunes
behind a chain-link barrier,
the bullets came flying and the beer bottles
crashed on the wall behind my head.

Once on the dance floor some dude
smacked his old lady to the ground.
Later that night she returned,
firing a .22 handgun into the bar
—and missing everybody—
as Little Willie G. crooned "Sad Girl"
from a turntable.

Con artists congregated here,
including the Earl of Lincoln Heights
who once sold a house he didn't own.

And boys with tattoos and scars crisscrossing skin
prowled the pool tables, passing bills,
while trying to out-hustle each other
as disco beats and *cumbias* pulled people
onto the lopsided dance floor.

My ex-wife danced too.
I watched dudes hold her, kiss her neck,
eye her behind
and look down
her sweaty breasts.

But I also knew this was the closest
I would ever get to her anymore,
in that dark corner,
with beer bottles rising from a table—
when she needed me.

Outside the Bull's Eye Inn
the hurting never stopped.

Outside the Bull's Eye Inn
we locked into hate
shrouded in the lips of love.

Outside the Bull's Eye Inn
we had two children
who witnessed our drunken brawls—
my boy once entered our room,
and danced and laughed with tears in his eyes
to get us to stop.

But inside, beside the blaze of bar lights,
she was the one who stole into my sleep,
the one who fondled my fears,
the one who inspired
the lust of honeyed remembrance.

She was the song of regret behind a sudden smile.

Peace

Keep your voice down, my husband
hissed this morning across his plate,
then knotted his tie
to a fist that would hold
all day. Wedged in our thin
walls against the silence of neighbors
we haven't met, I folded
my napkin, shoved the last word
back in my throat
and later jogged extra laps
as though my feet could make
some mark on firm ground,
could make everything clear.
I remove my damp
sweatclothes, shivering now
in the best boutique I can find.
An older woman shrugs out of a fur
soft as fog and gathers up jade, silver,
apple-green silks, all hushed
and viciously expensive.

She wraps herself in a gown
the color of doves, a shadow body
that follows no husband. I'm sure their house
holds a room where she dreams,
sends letters, while someone downstairs
seasons the greens and filets
and a reasonable hunger warms her like firelight.
If her children should quarrel
on the darkening lawn she drifts outside
to soothe each with a story, her voice adding
girth to itself like the wine,
open, breathing by his plate.

I want to ask for my size
in a gown like hers. I want to fill
a gown with breasts like hers, and move

through our rooms like a boat
through any water. I finger aqua silk
made for real hips and shoulders
I, too, could have after twenty seasons—

it turns a whole room blue
where I enter myself as I dress,
where my garments turn overhead light
back on itself like fine paintings.
Downstairs he slices meat striped with fat
and pink flesh, while I finger each
pearl on the choker he gave me when money
was tight. The blue folds drift
over my body, that house
filled with rooms left by daughters
and sons, that house given over
to pale silk and stone, its silence
my secret, my eyes raised
to meet hers in the triple mirror.

So Get Over It, Honey

First bout of Shanghai flu, sweat the bed without you
First night walking west over Ellington Bridge
spy Marilyn's face in the mural over HEIDI'S LIQUOR,
yearning, so I say, *Don't kill yourself* but this is ridiculous
without you
First conversation with my mother who tells me I'm selfish
without you
First movie I see, matinee about Monk whose wife and mistress
looked after him so he could play but still he cracked, he was a
genius without you
First Dorito binge 'til my lips turn into the slugs I poured salt on
when I was a kid without you
First talk-the-talk with Dave who says you're a schmuck so I
should go get laid without you
First drive to Carolina where my cousin Mason's wife takes the babies
and leaves the state and he crawls into detox—not easy, but simple
without you
First Christmas I wish I was Buddhist without you
First death, it was Dom, he was twenty-seven, lung cancer and that's
    all I know
without you
First time I tutor the kids at the shelter and say, *Tell me what you*
    like to do
and one says, *Go see Grandma* & the other says, *Stupid!*
    Grandma's dead
without you
First January thaw, I find a 1943 penny in the alley without you

First period, Oh there is a God without you

Hives

Hives, he told me, hives. I gave
him hives. Not HIV, not ulcers,
not herpes. Hives. Stress-
related hives, I gave him, over
the phone, one thousand miles away.
Hives that sent him into the hospital,
hooked to IV's, hives that sent
him reeling back to his girlfriend.

What power I have, conjuring hive
spells in my black purse, shaking
it to blend, unzipping to let loose
hive juice, spurting cross country!

It could have been worse for him.
I could have given him scurvy,
shingles, kwashiorkor. Rickets,
anemia, osteoporosis. He's lucky
I didn't choose sties, male pattern
baldness, boils on his buttocks,
canker sores. Not bunions, writer's
cramp, smegma, or tartar. I thought

about it hard. Hives. Just enough
discomfort to upset his routine. Just
enough ugliness to scare off his girlfriend.
I didn't count on his weak constitution,
wheezing, closed throat, inch-across welts.

I just didn't count. I didn't count. I didn't.

The Affair

1.

    Then the long fencerow, that years ago had
    heaved and buckled, took on a copper shine
    in the sunset, the dew. A garlic haze
    of cut pastures simmered fields away.

2.

    They were flushed from sex—they were
    traced with that other body, just parted.
    They stood in the length of first fall waiting.
    And their skin, that had been so willing,

3.

    delible as ash to trembling fingertip,
    became its own again. One star, three.
    Nothing good was going to happen. Night winds
    lifted themselves out of wheat rows and shook

4.

    off what had been done. So they turned
    elsewhere. Her fingers gathered up her collar
    softly in a bunch, and she put on a scarf.
    It was not even cold. It was only cool.

Marriage 2

One morning. I remember. My eyes steady, impartial.
I remember the individual dogwood blossoms,

the lazy ones, the eager; the drone
of a refrigerator; a windowshade's worrying tongue.

I could tell you how many dark bills were curled on our dresser,
even the dates of the brown pennies, still

warm from last night's palms. One morning, that morning,
the earth opened up. We fell into that gaping fissure. We kept

falling. I plunged past the ledge where the potion that said *husband*,
drink me, gleamed. This happened, was

happening, kept happening. I had just woken up, you
were about to, and me, pitched up on one elbow.

My God. What is more lovely than a man's head, curled
into his pillow? The swirls and eddies of his hair? His beard silently

growing into the morning? And what is more terrifying than your
love for him? All this happened. I heard a scratching at the door,
        was I so

wrong to think someone was coming to deliver me another life,
my real one? Was I so wrong to think when something dies,
        something else

is born? The plots of our lives do not match their themes. I left
you, I came back. Does this mean I might as well have never left

at all? Even now when I tell this story, the beginning and end
fit together, but the middle falls out. And that scratching?

Remember those 19th-century novels? Destiny used
to be so grand, so tragically instructive. Now, it comes nosing

its way into our bedrooms like a stupid puppy
to settle across our warm feet and teach us nothing.

At the Pioneer Valley Legal Clinic

All eyes are lowered
in the waiting room of my final visit.
Xerox machines whir,
operating like any human heart
by lights and memory
next time, next time, next . . .
From down the hall
a lecture sponsored by the Whiplash Club,
"Why Pain Does Not Make Us Special."

The clock ticks out Emergency
in minutes. All morning
I have carried what is left of my marriage
in a strongbox rusted, come
slightly unhinged.
It isn't heavy. Inside,
disappointment weighs nothing more
than, say, a child's pink bunny jacket
with its own two sleeves
tied together.

Now in the narrow
plastic seat hooked to all the others
as if this were an airport
or parochial school, I'm shifting, anxious
for what lies waiting
on the other side of a dotted line.
When a lawyer with hair blue as gunmetal bends close,
eyes full of rented grief,
I know what to do.

I say No Fault.
For once I do not call it train wreck, cruel
cosmic prank or house on fire.
I say, "I believe in precision
beyond blame, and second chances—
even those unasked for—

can be legal, binding."
I say, "Party of the first part."
I say, "We are all adults here," and when I do
parolees nodding off in the corner
moan a little, stirring,
the white perfume of documents
rising fiercely from their wrists.

After Skinnydipping, the Old Couple Fishes
for Brown Trout in the Root River

Peel back that thin top layer of the Earth's
skin and it might reveal a man
sitting alone in a diner
somewhere
on the Nebraska flood plain. Or
a woman flying
a kite in Arizona, a key
on her kite string to see
if electricity might find its thunder
on her blue
and cloudless day.
                Or better yet
an old woman and man casting
elk hair caddis and blue quill flies
toward the heart of
a Root River pool.
They have their hip waders on now
but nothing else. They try to sneak
glances at one another, let
their lines float with current.
Possibly it was long ago
they came to this place
and first took their bare chances
with loving, scattered rose
petals on the caramel-
colored water and then climbed
down its rungs and on
to each other where they've stayed
enough years
for their own pools to grow
full and rich with swirls.
So it seems sudden
              how
her rod tip bends,
a good trout on. When, finally,
she brings it to shore,

he bends down, lifts the fish
up from the river. They admire
quickly, as those
who have loved long
can, then give the trout back
to the place where its shadow has continued
breathing water and waiting.
The man kisses the woman's shoulder.
Her fingers flow along his chest.
                              On the shoregrass
pieces of clothing grow restless, bright rafts
unable to float
on their own.

The Embrace

You weren't well or really ill yet either;
just a little tired, your handsomeness
tinged by grief or anticipation, which brought
to your face a thoughtful, deepening grace.

I didn't for a moment doubt you were dead.
I knew that to be true still, even in the dream.
You'd been out—at work maybe?—
having a good day, almost energetic.

We seemed to be moving from some old house
where we'd lived, boxes everywhere, things
in disarray: that was the *story* of my dream,
but even asleep I was shocked out of narrative

by your face, the physical fact of your face:
inches from mine, smooth-shaven, loving, alert.
Why so difficult, remembering the actual look
of you? Without a photograph, without strain?

So when I saw your unguarded, reliable face,
your unmistakable gaze opening all the warmth
and clarity of you—warm brown tea—we held
each other for the time the dream allowed.

Bless you. You came back, so I could see you
once more, plainly, so I could rest against you
without thinking this happiness lessened anything,
without thinking you were alive again.

IV

IN THIS STRANGE LAND WE SING OUR SONG

Thoreau

My father and I have no place to go.
His wife will not let us in the house—
afraid of catching AIDS. She thinks
sleeping with men is more than a sin,
my father says, as we sit on the curb
in front of someone else's house.
Sixty-four years have made my father
impotent. Silver roots, faded black
dye mottling his hair make him look
almost comical, as if his shame
belonged to me. Last night we read
Thoreau in a steak house down the road
and wept: "If a man does not keep pace
with his companions, let him travel
to the music that he hears, however
measured or far away." The orchards
are gone, his village near Shanghai
bombed by the Japanese, the groves
I have known in Almaden—apricot,
walnut, peach, and plum—hacked down.

TV News: Detox Closed

No comment, just image after image
of the front line troops
in the Alcohol and Indian War—
The camera gives us back a day
with a band of merry tribal drunks
who, by midnight, will wind up
in ER, getting tested and typed,
paying in blood for a night's stay.

On a red carpeted stairway,
a TV newsman stands,
a polished bastard of a banister
glides thirty feet of wood
under his hand. He gazes
from the tube, ironic, amused,
saying that since Detox closed
taxpayers spend $300 per inebriate
on nightly emergency treatment.

He gestures meaningfully
at the parquet floor;
the chandelier winks
at his sick little joke
about the nightly rate
of a honeymoon suite,
which somehow explains
why he's reporting on Detox
from the foyer of a luxury hotel.

Yeah, I'd like to see those guys
put up for a night in the Ritz.
What a party! Sneak in some friends,
by the end of the night we'd drop
the taxpayers' cost to, say,
thirty dollars a head.

More video images, more faces.
I peer at them as through water,
wondering who they were on land.
Street Chiefs, I've heard them called,
a name whose honor is earned backward,
unspoken by the time it's deserved.
Heroes do return, yes, healed like warriors,
but these on TV are still so far away.

There is a battle in a distant country
where breath and drink are twins.
Each swallow, you pull toward that world
whose element is alcohol, not air.
Tilt the bottle to see the entrance,
a hole at the top of the sky, bright as sun,
the glass lip a tunnel toward that land
whose voice always provokes you
come on, come on,
where you belong —

Now tell me you wouldn't go.

Exquisite Candidate

I can promise you this: food in the White House
will change! No more granola, only fried eggs
flipped the way we like them. And ham ham ham!
Americans need ham! Nothing airy like debate for me!
Pigs will become the new symbol of glee,
displacing smiley faces and "Have A Nice Day."
Car bumpers are my billboards, billboards my movie screens.
Nothing I can say can be used against me.
My life flashes in front of my face daily.
Here's a snapshot of me as a baby. Then
marrying. My kids drink all their milk which helps the dairy industry.
A vote for me is not only a pat on the back for America!
A vote for me, my fellow Americans, is a vote for everyone like me!
If I were the type who made promises
I'd probably begin by saying: America,
relax! Buy big cars and tease your hair
as high as the Empire State Building.
Inch by inch, we're buying the world's sorrow.
Yeah, the world's sorrow, that's it!
The other side will have a lot to say about pork
but don't believe it! Their graphs are sloppy coloring books.
We're just fine—look at the way
everyone wants to speak English and live here!
Whatever you think of borders,
I am the only candidate to canoe over Niagara Falls
and live to photograph the Canadian side.
I'm the only Juilliard graduate—
I will exhale beauty all across this great land
of pork rinds and gas stations and scientists working for cures,
of satellite dishes over Sparky's Bar & Grill, the ease
of breakfast in the mornings, quiet peace of sleep at night.

Secret Asian Man

He's given a number,
he's given a new name,
he's given an automatic pistol,
he's given a license to kill.

He could be Chinese, Nepalese,
Cambodian, Timorese, Laotian,
Indonesian, Burmese, or Thai.

He can kick higher than Jackie Chan,
he can be devious as Dr. Fu Manchu,
he can speak better English than Charlie Chan,
and he can even make a great pot of Moo Goo Gai Pan.

He could be Korean, Japanese,
Singaporean, Malaysian, Tibetan,
Vietnamese, or from Brunei.

He'll torture you with drops of water between the eyes,
shove bamboo strips under your nails and dip them in iodine.
He'll torture you by tying you up in a wicker chair,
make you watch endless reruns of Kung Fu with David Carradine.

He's given a number,
he's given a new name,
he's given an automatic pistol,
he's given a license to kill.

Jimmy Pohoski's a Woman Now

The tank arsenal was only a few blocks away
from where I went to high school. Sometimes
we'd watch the tanks maneuvering on their track
and we'd know this made us tough, our eyes
on steel, our hearts set on Polish American girls
whose names it took us years to say right.

Jimmy Pohoski, one of us, has cut away
what set him apart from the Chevy dealer's daughter.
Where he used to breathe out, now
he inhales. He gets fired by a boss
who can't decide which employee restroom
Jimmy Pohoski should use, Jimmy whose eyes
singed the sides of tanks bound for Vietnam,
whose dreams must've embraced the likes
of Sonya Banascek and Dixie Styles
on Michigan summer nights when
you would hardly sweat
and could kiss with tongues as though the sky
would never get tired of holding you up.

Maybe I should remember this differently. Say
Jimmy Pohoski never showered with the rest of us
after phy. ed. class, that instead he sat in the darkest
of corners, staring at that "thing"
and trying to push it back, down
and in like the finger of an empty glove.
But all I can really see is some guy
scrawny and ugly like the rest of us, hoping
it would be what we would grow into
that counts, and maybe still does. There
we were, surrounded by the tool and die shops
of Ten Mile Road, the auto plants of Van Dyke
and Mound, a war everywhere we looked
and no Dixie in our arms.

I was told, even then, that what we love
will leave us. It could be some moment
so dramatic as the long flight across
a sea. Or so simple as a short climb
out of our lives. In the old neighborhood
we'd gather at the Pohoskis' side door, all of us
yelling "Yimmy, Yimmy" in unison, figuring
we'd go and watch the tanks roll
off the line, all of us soldiers, none of us
knowing we could lose, or that boys could grow
to become anything other than men.

Lingerie Ads in the Sixties

She is not there, except her body
is the specter in her Living

Underwear. She is ether,
air. See how she struts

her stuff, unsuckled nipples
pressing up against the lacy gauze

that seems to animate
pure lust. Liz Taylor

and her honeymooning breasts
lie out with Eddie on a beach

in France, but do we care
about these fleshpots

of the idle rich? Their tongues
are dust. A cleavage opens

between what we crave
and what we (bluntly)

are. Which is, perhaps, to say
that our unsullied heroine

is just where we would
want her, out of touch,

the eighteen-hour support she
promised but a ruse. Recall,

Madonna's still
a glint of silver

in her father's eye. Our girl
is not material. Ours

is wind, a slitted
sheath, a lie.

For the Jim Crow Mexican Restaurant in Cambridge, Massachusetts Where My Cousin Esteban Was Forbidden to Wait Tables Because He Wears Dreadlocks

I have noticed that the hostess in peasant dress,
the wait staff and the boss
share the complexion of a flour tortilla.
I have spooked the servers at my table
by trilling the word *burrito.*
I am aware of your T-shirt solidarity
with the refugees of the Américas,
since they steam in your kitchen.
I know my cousin Esteban the sculptor
rolled tortillas in your kitchen with the fingertips
of ancestral Puerto Rican cigarmakers.
I understand he wanted to be a waiter,
but you proclaimed his black dreadlocks unclean,
so he hissed in Spanish
and his apron collapsed on the floor.

May La Migra handcuff the wait staff
as suspected illegal aliens from Canada;
may a hundred mice dive from the oven
like diminutive leaping dolphins
during your Board of Health inspection;
may the kitchen workers strike, sitting
with folded hands as enchiladas blacken
and twisters of smoke panic the customers;
may a Zapatista squadron commandeer the refrigerator,
liberating a pillar of tortillas at gunpoint;
may you hallucinate dreadlocks
braided in thick vines around your ankles;
and may the Aztec gods pinned like butterflies
to the menu wait for you in the parking lot
at midnight, demanding that you spell their names.

When I Was White

When I was white I came and went, a cycle
of blood and moon and tide, hid nothing
of gun-shape inside me, debated evil

with no one. I said: Bring me something
handsome to eat and they did, that steak butter,
you could spread it on bread. I said: Bring

me taxis. They flew to my side and uttered
Get in and *Where to*, just the thing to carry me.
I said: We are all the same No Matter

What. This was my zaniest folly.
I had blinders on the sides of my head
big as real estate, blue as jelly. We

are all the same Underneath, I said,
and you could count the dusty liberals
nodding in deadly agreement, dead

as the Pope, dead as the Nazis, doornail
dead like the sunnies along Lake Michigan
and the poor bastard steadying his pole

ten feet up the beach. Jesus again,
this time with a sweet brown Chuckie B. face,
and I am beside you in the Bargain

Villa on Clark. I've traveled decades
through dead seas, I've seen my people flap
on their sides as they die of too much shade,

you can count them piling up on the maps
of the world, the unsightly word *equal*
a sticky drool from the Oh of their lips.

Black on Black

1.

    Night street an onyx eye unblinking, empty
but for him, black man, hood up,
coat too big, one hand deep in pocket.
Walks too fast, crossing toward me
I see now he's shaggy, 50 feet
and closing but still time for him
to look away, pull out a handkerchief,
too soon for me to jump to how
white people run from us.

    Twenty feet, eyes in the hood are on me,
his angle sharper, no mistake,
watch the hand, watch the hand, still in
that big pocket, street is blind,
shuttered, faceless, look for escape,
see small yard with gate,
close my hand on mace.

    Ten feet and he has not shaved, the parka is blue
with tattered fur, the hand is shoved to hell
down that huge pocket, in five seconds he will
draw forth flame, in five seconds he will
withdraw magnetic steel and make me slave
to gravity, his eyes are pulling for me,
his mouth about to move, make things official.

    Five feet and all sidewalk leads to him,
the hand now cranking from the pocket
like a steam shovel as his lips open,
the words will be the final kiss,
no time to mourn for lost brothers,
Move! I take the gate in three steps running,
make the yard, have gained 10 feet in snow
when his hand clears the pocket

to reveal a driver's license,
his ID, panhandling weapon against fear.

Not gonna rob you, sir, he says. Can you spare some change?

2.

Only after the elevator doors pinch off the night
does the attack come. I strike out, shout,
pound enameled walls for escape, but too late,
I am trapped in this bright cell
with a man who wears my clothes, jingles my keys
and spends our evenings
posing threats from doorway shadows,
holding soft lives hostage.
I have felt him follow me to entrances,
crossed streets against him,
scanned for him before parallel parking,
and handed him my wallet.
I have seen others shy from me
as from a disguised shark, shimmy past as if my hands
were hooks for women's purses.

Now here we are, two black men
within one skin, me alone in an elevator.
Me as the man who might have mugged me.
Me shoving myself against the wall,
blowing mirrors through my own brain.

Human Map

All quotes from "By Analyzing DNA Samples from 400 Ethnic Groups, Scientists Could Reconstruct Human History," Boyce Rensberger, Washington Post, *March 15–21, 1993*

You will be happy to know someone has asked our cells to tell,
in their own bloody language, whether or not all Indian tribes
descend from a single group that migrated from Asia.

Your own body contains the answer and the map: "Hidden within
the DNA of each human being is a record of that person's ethnic
  history."
Just one drop can read like a mystery.

All the way back to "humanity's dim evolutionary past,"
without a flashlight, scientists can trace
"the ancient migrations and ancestral intermixings
that have shaped every tribe and culture on Earth."

Still, it's too late to test Sky Woman, whose breath of life exists
in all creatures, or Thought Woman, who imagines us even now,
or any of the First Beings who survived by tricks.

Too late, so they will have to settle for *your* blood.

Some tribal jokesters call this *The Vampire Project.* Rumor has it
donations need no consent and any clinic might be in on it—so
go ahead—Give Blood! It's your civic duty.

Anthropologists, our old friends, support this "needy and urgent
cause." And who knows? You may be one of the "HIP people"
(Historically Interesting Population)
who, they note, are vanishing at an alarming rate.

Vanishing? They make it sound so passive, as if whole peoples
simply fade away.

You say you won't go to the blood drive? But the needle's nothing
new. Bloodshed always determines who inherits a patch of earth.
Even they admit their findings might be used to support
"increasingly incendiary claims of land tenure in ethnic disputes."

Do not fear this genetic tattooing—if they keep it up long enough
they will discover we all belong to one mother.

Scholars insist "the concept of race long ago lost its scientific
validity." And you know how well the general public embraces
these subtle distinctions and complex genetic notions.
Soon racism *as we know it* will end.

Whether we help them or not is no matter. Our blood will out.
Our bodies' code will crack. They will have their map.

To the Moon, Alice

Last night the man next door tried to throw the woman
next door with an emphasis more on distance
than accuracy while she dug something
of a Marianas Trench in his back that was not

as deep but redder than the original of which
I've seen color-enhanced Landsat photos. Who decides
whether blue's more important than orange
as a conveyance of depth or if the man next door

should continue in that capacity or be promoted
to the con in the next cell who sings Roy Orbison
badly? By this morning some progress
had been made in the arena of these decisions

based on the logic that if two people
of murderous intent are stored in a tight space
over a long period of time they must
eventually learn to select the floral pattern

in something approaching domestic accord. Today
a flurry of Florence Nightingale behavior
includes kisses for the bruise and cut
and the forehead behind which the image

of the chair lifted and bottle thrown still
flares with that nagging incapacity of memory
to rewrite terror as grace. For her there will be
roses, lamb stew with stunted potatoes

and crystallized garlic for him and for both a case
of beer will christen the days when *thank you
honey it's time for your distemper shot
dear* is just a pinch of the treacle they'll stun

each other with. Other inevitables are gravity
and dirt and the resurgence of an ineffective
radical left in American politics to give
the majorities in Durham and Omaha

something to wipe off their boots each November.
There will come another Saturday night
when a section of drywall's confirmed
to be less durable than Samsonite

and the tenacity of hair's proven by foot-pounds
of torque or some fashion of metal
enters flesh at one of the dainty junctures,
after which a judge will instruct a jury to ignore

the defense attorney's allusions to passion
and just focus on the law. For now he's back
and bandaged and mowing, she's inside
and singing to the sewing machine as repairs

continue, I'm at my desk and the trees are poised
for eventual collapse and love is what they feel
and love is what they defend and what
but love follows the corpse to the lovely grave?

The Man Who Tried to Rape You

When he appears a block away, you know.
Like when you watch a made-for-TV movie
and guess the ending in a minute,

or how, if you're listening, you'll almost hear
a pulse, a muted beat inside your head,
announcing the return of what's been coming.

Surprisingly, you think, it takes the form
of what's most obvious: the backlit shape
of trouble—first a faceless outline,

as if whoever drew this couldn't find
the way to fill it in, the buzzing mist
of streetlamps making ghosts of all his edges.

And then that ghost you've always feared is coming,
is walking toward you up the sidewalk, up
from childhood and books and all the movies

with which you've ever scared yourself, purposeless
as ghosts are, vaguely sad and understanding
in a way, as if he, too, knows a thing

about what's inevitable. The pause
before he grabs for you is awkward as
a school dance. It's like that, you think, a dance:

his arms heavy at your waist, the way he
smells not unpleasant, pulls you toward
his hips, which, in another case, might please

or thrill you. But now that thrill is fear, or
maybe it always was. The dance goes on
a moment more and you're not screaming, only

saying *No* and *No* and *No*; this becomes
a rhythm, like breathing, just as quiet,
as if you'll go on saying *No* forever,

and then he stops. Lets go. You wonder later
if it's your business to be generous.
And that you're sad and frightened, but not angry.

And where he went, pathetic silhouette,
the man who walked away, back to the dark;
how, after, even streetlamps seemed too bright

to fall on him. His face turning away.

Bearing Witness

—for Jacki B.

If you have lived it, then
it seems I must hear it.
—Holly Near

When the long-fingered leaves of the sycamore
flutter in the wind, spiky
seed balls swinging, and a child throws his aqua
lunch bag over the school yard railing, the last thing,
the very last thing you want to think about
is what happens to children when they're crushed
like grain in the worn mortar of the cruel.

We weep at tragedy, a baby sailing
through the windshield like a cabbage, a shoe.
The young remnants of war, arms sheared and eyeless,
they lie like eggs on the rescue center's bare floor.

But we draw a line at the sadistic,
as if our yellow plastic tape would keep harm
confined. We don't want to know
what generations of terror do to the young
who are fed like cloth
under the machine's relentless needle.

In the paper, we'll read about the ordinary neighbor
who chopped up boys; at the movies we pay
to shoot up that adrenaline rush—
and the spent aftermath, relief
like a long-awaited piss.

But face to face with the living prey,
we turn away, rev the motor, as though
we've seen a ghost—which, in a way, we have:
one who wanders the world,
tugging on sleeves, trying to find the road home.

And if we stop, all our fears
will come to pass. The knowledge of evil
will coat us like grease
from a long shift at the griddle. Our sweat
will smell like the sweat of the victims.

And this is why you do it—listen
at the outskirts of what our species
has accomplished, listen until the world is flat
again, and you are standing on its edge.
This is why you hold them in your arms, allowing
their snot to smear your skin, their sour
breath to mist your face. You listen
to slash the membrane that divides us, to plant
the hard shiny seed of yourself
in the common earth. You crank
open the rusty hinge of your heart
like an old beach umbrella. Because God
is not a flash of diamond light. God is
the kicked child, the child
who rocks alone in the basement,
the one fucked so many times
she does not know her name, her mind
burning like a star.

Evidence of Death's Voodoo—Inside
and outside the "Gun as Art Exhibit"

I'm in black leather, the guns are wrapped in string, tape, wire,
and cloth.

WWII, my mother worked in a munitions factory.

Klansman holds his gun like a broadsword.

After watching *The Essential Beatles* video, my thirteen-year-old
is desolate. "I wish they'd get back together," she says.

Women with guns: Gail with a .45 caliber Colt Gold Cup; Libby
with her 380 Sigsaur.

Sometimes the flat dull gunmetal dumbness of it all gets to me.

Under an illustration: "Dick said, 'Stop, Jane, don't touch the gun.'"
—*"happiness is a warm gun. . . .*

Mornings, I gulp premarin and prozac, cognitive Molotov cocktail.

At lunch, at the mall, we all order chicken fingers and joke about
human fingers.

Photo caption: "I'm gonna beat you like a stepchild."

Somewhere, someone makes it his business to manufacture
POLICE EVIDENCE tape and POLICE EVIDENCE tags.

> *bang, bang, shoot, shoot"*—

Theoretical bullet trajectories: through a banana; through an
apple; through a headless, human torso.

Termites. A friend suggests I paint each with the name of an
enemy before I call in the exterminators.

So help me. At the thought of this. I laugh.

Columbine High School/Littleton, CO

Here, thirteen high school students died,
murdered by two other high school students
—the memorial consists
of fifteen crosses. In this photograph, a woman
rests her head against one upright beam
as if decanting
(*trying* to) everything that's in her brain
—only the wood, only something
inhuman now, could hold what flows from her.
This grief's too vast for us, a color of its own,
not from our limited strip of the spectrum.
Really all that makes this picture comprehensible
to us—to we who view, but haven't
lived, this news—is the take-out cup
for her cola. You know, with the plastic lid
and the straw. A summer movie
advertised around it. Droplets
on the side, from where its ice and the heat
of the afternoon commune.
It's large. You've had it
on maybe a thousand occasions. Any of us
might hold this drink,
might take it into our systems.

Blood

Sometimes blood looks for an opening,
any way to get out from under us and the knives.
Blood cuts into blood to look and its hands grasp blood.
My block is a corral of yellow crime scene tape.
Twenty cop cars—
sometimes blood looks at blood for an explanation.
It turns out the whole block slept through a murder.
A social worker was stabbed by her psychotic charge
not two houses down, near the door of the Headstart School,
where the underprivileged play catch-up next door to the door to the
     School for the Disabled.
Both schools are underfunded, with all their school-day lives.
Call us childish, call us to our teachers:
a cop with a clipboard calls me over, to ask me what of blood I heard.
He knows in his blood better than to say it that way.
He puts it neutrally, may his heart feel adjudged by restraint,
may the differently abled be restrained for their own good,
and when I say *his* "heart" may I mean *mine* and may my mouth
     feel antique—
what he asks me is if I heard any cries—no, not even that, just . . .
     "anything."
Let's get this right.
Does a dying self make up a face as it goes, will any face do?
Right there on the concrete a bloodstain the children will pass, to
     touch it:
what's to touch once blood stops doing its cartwheels?
Someone has stepped out from under our thumbs and heels?
I wish I had a heart that would take care of . . . what?
Can anyone ever make blood do anything? Can clouds be pushed
     around?
On and on till the questions are all open coffins.
Sleepy me, a cop, a schizo the state sent packing
and a dead do-gooder the papers will leach till her photo is a
     window after death.
By the windows of institutional ministration the cop
glances away from me at wheelchairs, spokes aglitter
like Ezekiel's chariot about to commence his convictions.

God cares that our families and homelands are slaughtered for
    being weak.
We are all victims, down to the butchers among us?
Weakness has strength, even if it hasn't killed us?
Coffins.
I drive by these windows each day, some strapped in headgear,
others who can be trusted to walk careen from wall to wall—
one always laughs with a "it's not funny" lodged in his laugh;
another always carries a Raggedy Ann doll with a sewed smile
and button eyes hanging by threads,
the stuffing coming out of it, affection has mauled it—
she holds tight what even oblivion gave up torturing,
clouds shining, her wheelchair passes me, a cop and our laws and
    our clue, blood;
its driver squints smiling into a happiness that is its own skewed
    warding of us off,
her wheelchair shines—O steel throne—a fool might even believe
she would wish to reign over our disabling kingdom.

And we came home

to the bloody village,
to whole streets of loss,
   whole rooms,
saying what passed for prayer

because we did not know
how to live in the new world,
   and I would take you,
who are my rose inside me blossoming,

back to where the sidewalks
are so wide for promenade,
   what the French abandoned,
like their mistresses

and their architecture
haunted by the savage rule of class,
   gentlemen who'd hanged their brothers
in the doorways of another time.

We could walk down Nguyen Du Street
beside the lake,
   then follow the lost trolley tracks
back to old Hanoi

and find the seven ancient gates
to save at least their memory. No one
   understands how we felt.
Kill it all. Kill it all.

To the Vietnam Vet

It must have been like a funhouse,
walking the high cliffs under rock apes,
dodging the large stones they tossed down,
lifting the black death to shoo them,
when the women were as cheap as cigarettes,
dutiful, lasting as long as the dollars.
In the jungle night must have felt like
the plumage of a giant peacock around you,
a billion eyes still as pursed lips on
your arms. I remember this when I approach
your house on foot, peeking under cedar
bushes for feet other than the slanting trunk,
taking cover under the first lamplight.
When you peek from your window smeared with
paint, I know it is you and not the black
patriot sleeping in shit with dead men,
remembering Martha & The Vandellas,
afraid to call out to soldiers who
declared it was not your war. Strange
thing when they fire vets from jobs because
they remember, because they stand still
for a moment like sailors tied to a mast,
weathering the storm of phantoms. Stranger
still that I must write a hundred songs
for your unpainted army because I want
you all to believe I understand.

Facing It

My black face fades,
hiding inside the black granite.
I said I wouldn't,
dammit: No tears.
I'm stone. I'm flesh.
My clouded reflection eyes me
like a bird of prey, the profile of night
slanted against morning. I turn
this way—the stone lets me go.
I turn that way—I'm inside
the Vietnam Veterans Memorial
again, depending on the light
to make a difference.
I go down the 58,022 names,
half-expecting to find
my own in letters like smoke.
I touch the name Andrew Johnson;
I see the booby trap's white flash.
Names shimmer on a woman's blouse
but when she walks away
the names stay on the wall.
Brushstrokes flash, a red bird's
wings cutting across my stare.
The sky. A plane in the sky.
A white vet's image floats
closer to me, then his pale eyes
look through mine. I'm a window.
He's lost his right arm
inside the stone. In the black mirror
a woman's trying to erase names:
No, she's brushing a boy's hair.

Exquisite Communist

Their world is red banners and small potatoes,
soft rotten ones sprouting eyes.
Doctors and plumbers are paid the same
as dogwalkers. Everyone wears brown and loden green.
Even the children blossom in shades of tan.
The sky is a gray metal file cabinet,
the stars full of spy secrets.
Once the tallest building in the Bronx
was the Russian building. It leaned as the government leaned
into China or Vietnam. The computers were big
and old and not very good, statues the color of mold,
their genitals shrunken, frozen, sorrowful.
There is one Communist left in New York City. Her name is Sam
and she would prefer it if you gave your leftovers
to the neighbors. If she were president
someone would probably murder her instantly,
in her sleep, and she'd never get media coverage.
I did my eighth grade social studies report on Communism.
I like the ideas, though I never got around to becoming one.

Cement Cloud

—for Reesom Haile & Saba Kidane

Front window TV breaking news just breaking
Lucy at the assembly line. Must eat more pastries faster!
When One falls, I think if the Other comes this way
It would flatten my flat yet Dad waits for family to come
Home what is that a place of safety laughter breaks
The sky so clear and how beautifully plunging my Friends
From the flaming pickets of the "World" nefarious
Brilliance blinds from death even "Is the air controller's
Computer broken or what?" asks the newscaster when news
Is history lies jokes tell themselves leaving trails of skin

The panic from just outside is my story holes of plane
Flames of symbol clocks of hearts the ash and human
And human there is first the body keep telling yourself
That or anything because what comes next to LIFT us
Ineffable dies in the utter unspeakability political under
Standing or taking of everything the value of freedom
Of peace and the seed that grows into a home where
The door can open a fireball erupts your tongue
Is suddenly singing Remember eyes locked forever
On the double tombstone that is not there and always

———

Dear Friends—we're camping out on Duane St w/o phone/electric
but lives yes just live em till till, I guess. I'm at my dear brother's
office on 20th St—Internet, phone, hooray!

Yesterday, Elizabeth looked me in the eye and said, Do not withdraw!
The first time anyone's ever had the nerve to say that to me (the other
side of my maniae, donchaknow). It was amazing to hear. I heard.
And I recommend it to everyone. Do not withdraw!

The horrors are everywhere; it is incomprehensible. It is bitter and ugly and sad and the concrete—the streets they are the same but what's on them now are vehicles of death and pollution, of clean up and try to wash off the stench of destruction. This is hard to imagine in my City, my beautiful City full of energy and sharp beauty.

The smell is powerful, acrid; masks are important. I ride my bike, checkpoint at 14th is calm, Houston is tough, Canal varies. I have not walked below Duane. The rubble of 7WTC still smolders at the end of Greenwich St, 5 blocks away.

Rumors fly about why there's no electric—gas leaks was the leading reason until I turned on my gas and it worked. The giant floodlights at night maybe?—they get direct hooks, perhaps that's why the neighborhood's unplugged.

Hard to do anything. I missed my class at Bard on Wednesday but I do find the books we're reading (Eco's *The Island of the Day Before* and Frank Standord's *The Battlefield Where the Moon Says I Love You*) soothing.

One thing—we don't think of when things will return to Normal. There's a new normal now, with tentacles in many directions and time is needed to grip them, for them to grip us and each other. Don't withdraw. Use words.

The Way Things Used to Be

When we moved out here thirty years ago there weren't so many paved roads. There were fewer houses, fewer people. There weren't so many lights. Could be there's more of everything now. It seems to me we get more snow now than we used to. We were a long way from town in those days but we didn't see so many animals. There were tracks, only suggestions. . . . I'm sure we see more moose nowadays. It was quiet. There was the wind in the spruce trees that seemed sometimes as if it were saying something, but wasn't. Often on clear nights you'd see the aurora. Basically, though, there was nothing out here. That's changed. It's hard to explain the way things used to be. It's hard to find words to explain the loss of nothing.

Heaven

Between my back fence and the drainage ditch,
the county's
                no man's land, I'd been chopping brush
and forking out
                thick roots—some extra room
for bush beans and potatoes. Had been.
                        I'd stopped.
Before me,
        coiled in weeds,
                a copperhead
jabbed at
        my boots, but I could barely feel it.
Tap tap. I didn't move. A copperhead,
and I could barely feel it!
                I'd armored myself
in long pants, work
            gloves, rubber boots
against
        this weaponed patch of wilderness:
thorns, yellow jackets, nettles, poison oak,
and wild
        blackberry cane—the
                serpent's Eden,
the copperhead's paradise,
                which I had cleared,
hoed into furrows, planted. The brown
                head struck,
bit,
    fought my rubber boots till I could feel,
with joy,
        how much he hated me,
and with the hoe, I hooked
            the angry snake

and flicked it,
              writhing, across the ditch
into my neighbor's untouched bramble, where
the gray squirrels, rabbits, mice
                          had also fled
from my blade, my
              advancing paradise.

A Star Is Born in the Eagle Nebula
— *to Larry Levis, 1946–1996*

They've finally admitted that trying to save oil-soaked
seabirds is tougher than it looks. You can wash them, rinse them
with a high-pressure nozzle, feed them activated charcoal
to absorb toxic chemicals & test them for anemia, but the oil
still disrupts the microscopic alignment of feathers that creates
a kind of wet suit around the body. We now know that the caramel
coloring in whiskey causes nightmares, & an ingredient in beer
produces hemorrhoids. Glycerol in vodka causes anal seepage,
& when girls enter puberty, the growth of their left ventricles
slows down for about a year. Box office receipts plummeted
　　this week.
Retail sales are sluggish. The price of wheat rose. Soybeans sank.
The Dow is up thirty points. A man named Alan Gerry has bought
Woodstock & plans to build a theme park, a sort of combo
Williamsburg/Disneyland for graying hippies. The weather report
predicts a batch of showers preceding a cold front down
on the Middle Atlantic Coast—you're not missing much.
Day after day at the Ford research labs in Dearborn, Michigan,
an engineer in charge of hood latches labors, measuring the weight
of a hood, calculating the resistance of the latch, coming up
with the perfect closure, the perfect snapping sound,
while the shadow of Jupiter's moon, Io, races across cloud tops
at 10.5 miles a second, and a star is born in the Eagle Nebula.
Molecular hydrogen and dust condenses into lumps that contract
and ignite under their own gravity. In today's paper four girls
in a photo appear to be tied, as if by invisible threads, to five
soap bubbles floating along the street against the black wall
of the Park Avenue underpass. Nothing earthshattering. The girls
are simply *there*. They've blown the bubbles & are following them
up the street. That's the plot. *A life. Any life.* I turn the page,
and Charlie Brown is saying—"Sometimes I lie awake at night
& ask, 'Does anyone remember me?' & a voice comes to me
out of the dark, 'Sure, Frank, we remember you.'"

Future Debris

The typical object up there is about the size of a filing cabinet.
— *"Space Junk a Danger to Launches,"* Johns Hopkins Gazette,
August 23, 1988

Until he died we thought our neighbor dull.
Now he's a distant point of light.
His cremated body orbits low
in its reflectorized canister creating
what the space burial firm called
"a twinkling reminder of the loved one."
There's a wheel chart to map his course.
Nights we go around back of the house,
gaze at what little true sky winks
through the haze of debris.
It amazes me and is a relief, really,
not to have the whole universe
smack up against me like a wall.
All my life I've strained to comprehend
planets and motion, all the unending
that's been clouded, obscured
by the detritus humans seem to produce
naturally, ink to the squid, protective
cloak through which we cannot see
and therefore feel we are not seen.
Some night, a little girl, who will know
only tame animals, city trees, will listen
to my tales of wilderness and game.
I'll hold her up so she basks in the glint
of celestial jetsam. She will spread her hands,
reach for the bright flecks, ask if they are wild.
Lying to the child, I'll say they are. Then the filing
cabinets, ah, they'll glimmer like stars!

Sping

Is the straw
and the camel and its back
and the last haystack in which
the poison needle is found.

Spring is the exact number of times it will take
until the small, aging man snaps
the haranguing wife, boss, friend, lover
finds the hatchet, tire iron, hammer, blade.
How the kerosene, torch are located.

How Rosa Parks found her bus seat.
Spring is the dustbowl and Black Tuesday.
Spring is the dodo and passenger pigeon packing up.
How the child was found in the well.
Spring is the Code of Hammurabi and the Fifth Amendment.
Spring cannot always be trusted.

Sping = x when x is why?
Spring is greater than city hall.
Sping is why waves and wherefores break
        the waves mounting into revolution arguments
        the shore receding until Ushers fall
        the critical mass of starlings, the breakpoint
        of white tigers, the avalanche of the zebra mussel
            the zeitgeist of
                pterodactyls and monsoon winds

all begin with Spring.

This tiny prime cannot be divided.
"I just couldn't take it anymore."
It is the personal number of those put aside
        putting aside, putting aside
a binominal in the formula
of real and imagined victims and

it is enough.

Rajah in Babylon

We hanged our harps upon the willows in the midst thereof.
—*Psalm 137*

Rajah doesn't like Nirvana but he seems
to tolerate Jimmy Cliff: "The Harder They Come"

is Rachel's little joke, and it's chuffing from her boom box
as Rajah paces, his planetary back-

and-forth, manic orbits, exactly like Rilke's
panther. The bars and his stripes run parallel

and fuse, head abob like a marionette's,
the snare drum of his paws on the cement.

He's fasted for three days, and thinks that Rachel's
brought ten pounds of horse meat in her pail,

but his flared puzzled nostrils don't smell a thing
and Noelle bends down to the tranquilizer gun

while Rachel coos endearments meant
to slow him down so Noelle will get a decent shot.

Good Rajah Pretty Rajah Big Rajah —
Eyes wide, he turns, and Noelle aims and fires

and he shrieks and circles faster and we wait
while Jimmy croons that we can get it if we really want.

"Two minutes, tops," says Rachel, and by the time
the song is over he has wobbled and gone down.

He is one four-thousandth of the world's tigers.
To save them takes some drastic measures

and so the cage door's opened and we file
in, Bob and Noelle and Rachel

and me, and the tape slurs on to "Pressure Drop"
while Bob and Noelle strain to turn him on his back,

heaving till he's sprawling belly up,
the Maytals moaning as Rachel wipes

her brow, and fumbles with the electro-jack,
a miniature land mine, a low-tech

bristle of hose and wire. The down-sheathed penis
sprouts, pink and man-sized in her rubber gloves

and low the Melodians lay down beside
the rivers of Babylon. *Oh the wicked*

carried us away, captivity . . . The motor's
started, the penis clamped, the tiger

bright burning, his fearful symmetry
sprawled incandescent on the scat-pocked floor. Gingerly

I touch the ribs, the whorled sleeping flank,
stutter of heartbeat, Rachel scowling as she works,

and there we wailed as we / remembered Zion.
And slowly the liquid pearls in the flask, churn

and sputter as Rachel grins. Buttermilk
gold, *and there we wailed*, it streaks

the beaker's glassy walls, brimming and bound
for dry-ice burial, for resurrection in the wild,

Sumatra and some sleeping tigress. *By Babylon
we wailed.* Applause and the Melodians

fade. The bright liquid flares. *Oh Jerusalem,
in this strange land we sing our song.*

V

THE STRENUOUS WORK OF VANISHING

Estrogen

One day I too will be
found, a lightning root
in a sky underground,

marked by whatever the years
will have done—the fur
my hands have stroked, the greens

that pushed through soil
and passed my lips,
the darkness my bones carried

and yes, something
glittering in the champagne
those nights I thought I would live

forever, petal that I was.
The wind wrapped me in a skein of cries.
I aged closer to the ground

and fell in with the weather as she
changed and changed her mind.
My breasts ached.

Then shrank. My bones
thinned to lace. Was this
a departure? Some

would have it so — some
who walk the world with one
blind eye and one empty socket.

Variation on a Sundial

The first time I ever got a really good fix on time,
How slowly it moved, how absolutely blunt
And inconsiderate of it not to pass, was in a field,

Nearly lunch. Since dawn, with brutally surgical
Hoes, we had been thinning the young cotton,
And I remember thinking, If I was a boy with a friend

A year older, and he had a friend a year older,
And he had a friend a year older, then we were all
Together in this: the old man Bill, whose father

Had fought at Chickamauga, and the prophet
Ezekiel, and the girl Shirley with snot caramelized
In her nostrils. But in the shade of scuppernong

The sandwiches stayed distant as Nebuchadnezzar.
The rows went ahead and behind and pray, tell me,
What do you plan to do to stop thinking of sleep

When you cannot sleep? On clear days in June
You can make a clock by drawing a circle in the dirt.
If you drive a stick precisely at the origin,

The hour will fall as the shadow of that stick.
You can count the steps to the end of the row. You
Can sing, but the shadow never gets to twelve.

That is the meaning of Zeno's paradox: I would learn
This in the fall of 1970, at the University of Alabama,
In J. D. McMinn's Elements of Western Philosophy,

A semester I wasted, for I would also learn from drugs,
From songs, from the long minutes of short years,
Doing everything three times since I was a Protestant.

I would try very hard to see the present as it changed.
But there where the dark print merged with the dark
And I threw down the book, not marking the place;

There with the tongue which is the prayer of the kiss;
And there above cliffs when I shook my head madly
From side to side and slapped myself to stay awake;

It was not here yet or it was gone. No one told me
I would not know it, for there would not be time,
And from such omissions, the decades would evolve.

Kansas

If a lifetime is North America then I have reached Kansas.
From here I can see it all coming. Hail? Moving this way
from the next town, the girl has dropped all the white marbles
out of her apron. Twisters? I watch them from far off,
meandering old women bending at the waist,
berry picking. Their deep blue aprons are full
of everything that can be plucked and taken away.
Fierce gray hair flying, they can drive
a two-by-four like a golden needle through the pink silk
belly of a sow. I see Joe the Reaper, a sweet slack-jawed
boy who's too good at his work, never misses a stalk or a beat,
sweeps it all flat to the ground. Behind me, due east?
Love, its cracked voiceless bell, its proclamations and declarations,
its lobster traps, buttery pots, thwacking harpoons, its Shaker
    furniture,
quivering on bony legs like a newborn colt. Behind me, the restraint
of small black buckled shoes, behind me—*that God.* In front?
Solitude, the great desolation. Hawkish, I am
a stalked stalker. Old, with my knife, my red bowl, my funnel,
my great black apron. Alone, thirsting. In front of me is where
I will cut the arm from a cactus and finally taste the green juice
I've imagined my whole life, the wonderful thirst, the bitter
    quenching.
I walk, into the scribblings of sidewinders, the screeching of birds
with bloody beaks, the sun, her dress on fire, lowering herself
into the salty arms of her blue, undrinkable, moaning lover,
    screaming,
shaking the earth, breaking up the furniture. That God.

At the Hairdresser, Reading *Elle* Magazine

Each year the models get younger
and younger, disappear when you look
at them sideways. Beneath the silvery, bubbled bonnet
of the hair dryer my brown hair "processes,"
my whole head covered with a sticky paste

the color of raisins, that covers any stray
grey strands and brings out my natural red highlights.
"Grey-Be-Gone," my hairdresser calls it,
though in truth it seems no different
from my stepmother's Lady Clairol,

> *hair color so natural*
> *only your hairdresser knows for sure.*

My hairdresser knows. I flip through the pages
as the models parade down spring runways
in Paris, New York, in Rome, like exotic birds
about to take off in clothes no real woman could wear.
Once there was a time when I could make a skirt

out of a yard of fabric. Pink velvet one New Year's,
and a shadow-striped white voile bodyshirt
that showed slats of shining skin, my ovaries bursting
like ripe pomegranates with their plenty.
Now, erratic hormonal buzzes—wasps trapped

inside a storm window in winter.
Everything dies. And I know some of these models
starve for a living, their angular, nearly hipless shapes
a reminder of my own, the finger down my throat all sophomore year.
Then, out of nowhere, my grandmother's beautiful

ravaged face the last time I saw her alive, the high, rouged
cheekbones and delicate skull shining from the arthritic
wreck of her body, until the room where she lay on her chaise
of rose-colored silk seemed to glow, and we weren't anywhere
but in our bodies—my aunt, my grandmother, and me—

the red in my hair the same as the red had been in theirs,
the young woman I still am leaning toward them
(as, for a moment, the models lean from their glossy pages
    toward me),
breathing while the world breathed with us, understanding
for the space of a heartbeat, time's sweet and invincible secret:

that everything repeats, and we watch it. We watch it.

Losing My Hair

How can I walk outside without its springs
to bounce the sun back from my face?
How can I take my blind mother to church
and be seen as her life's potent continuation,
if hair stops doing copper pushups on my head?

How can I survive beautiful girls' eyes
with no curls crackling, "I'm full of fire for you!"
How can I not, at work, seem foolish middle-
aged (must middle age always seem foolish?)
If no Birds of Promise nest above my brain?

Soft roof of the body's mansion—sleek
fur hat—pine-needled carpet covering
my bright ideas—protein extrusions,
helping me build happy times—
how can I order a Big Mac and feel kin

to the checkout girl, and not the dour drudge
with his name tag: Hank Skelley, Manager?
How can I start my car with a boyish
wrist flick? How can I fly coach class
to Denver, not mistaken for a mortal

who, if his plane crashed, could die?
Bring me potions, grafts, weavings, wigs,
gene therapy! How else can I get back
my seat in seventh grade? How else can I
hunt Easter Eggs, rejoin the Pee Wee League,

claim my half-price movie tickets,
my child's plate? Crown, miter, headdress
of youthful office, what should I do?
My head's a planet with failing gravity.
One by one its people fall into the sky.

The Sexual Revolution

In that time of great freedom to touch
    and get in touch,
we lived on the prairie amid polite

moral certainty. The sensate world seemed
    elsewhere, and was.
On our color television the president's body

admitted he was lying. There was marching
    in the suddenly charged streets,
and what a girl in a headband and miniskirt

called *communication*. A faraway friend wrote
    to say the erotic life
was the only life. Get with it, he said.

But many must have been slow-witted
    during The Age of Enlightenment,
led artless lives during The Golden Age.

We watched the revolution on the evening news.
    It was 1972
when the sixties reached all the way

to where we were. The air became alive
    with incense and license.
The stores sold permission and I bought

and my wife bought until we were left
    with almost nothing.
Even the prairie itself changed;

people began to call it the Land, and once again
    it was impossibly green
and stretched endlessly ahead of us.

Epitome Café

Two pennies my change for a cup of Kona Blue, a pricey dive for
exotic brews and batiked children, pierced and haltered, performing
a costume drama of my youth. Their dreads nod in kindly approval
of my presence, my age forgiven me, my tablet the badge that lets
me trespass among them. They plot high jinx and map a path to
tragic credentials and well-placed scars.

Ah, my karmic darlings, stillness is the way, even on the postmodern
road. With effortless arrival, the weight of years will mark you, bend
you to its arc. Look: it has cost me nothing, this passage *gratis*. Listen
as I count you the price: flood and cyclone, a father's demise, the child
cast out, the unnatural disaster of her pummeled face. Approach at
your peril and kiss my brow. Feel the flame that persists, the love
unbid, igniting ash.

The Young

The young are wrong about love. It's not that they all say
The same thing about it. They have so many different ideas;
They think about their fathers and mothers, they think
About how they felt in high school, they don't live at home
Anymore, and they're scared but they can't show it.

The young want love too much. They think it will help
Them understand. You can see the young in phone booths
Talking about love. You can see them in small cars, waving
Their arms, both hands off the wheel to show how brave
They are about love. They want to be brave, they're learning.

The young start trouble when they fall in love. They write
Poems about blood and broken goblets. They wait late at night
For those who never come. If you could peek in the window,
You'd see how angry they are. If you could stand outside
On the balcony, you'd hear them screaming, I won't, I won't.

Some of the young say love is only a way of thinking
About love. They decide to think what they want about it,
But they don't have much to go on. That's why you can find
The young staring disconsolately out coffeehouse windows.
They're wondering what it feels like to know when you're

In love, and they think they ought to be able to tell.
They order café mocha, they drink the strong chocolate,
They think about the gestures of lovers, they imagine
The bodies of men and women, their faces are serious,
They wrap both hands around the hot glass of café mocha.

The young want someone to die of love. They mean no harm,
They're curious, wondering about the way it would happen.
They don't like to believe in suicide, they wonder if there's
Another way, with love like a serum that only makes you
Tired at first, but then you die of it, painlessly.

The young want to be everywhere at once. That's why
They're saved from dying of love. You can see them make
Their escape, their lean bodies darting into life.
They're sure they'll have other chances. They're sure
To forget. They have so long, and they don't yet know.

Priestess of Love

I wanted to be a priestess of love,
angel of mercy, crystal in a sun-streaked window
staining the world, a dark red valentine pressed
between the pages of a schoolboy's book, an obscure
poem about water, wind, stone, heat
of sun on rock, a musk-scented grove of fern.
Instead I drew psychedelic patterns
on my toes with colored marker and flaunted
them through my leather thongs
at my best friend's older brother
when he took us in his yellow mustang to hear the burning
cool flute of Herbie Mann. I wanted
to cover myself with paint and roll on canvas,
make art with the instrument I loved best,
my virginal body with its swelling breasts,
twin pelvic bones delicately protruding on either side
of my barely risen belly. Like the moist,
searching tongue of a deer stripping bark
from a sapling I thirsted for the world,
like tiny bubbles in champagne
I rose and crested,
waiting to overflow.

Wildflowers

In nineteen hundred sixty five
    the planets wobbled out of orbit,

red-winged blackbirds chanted Hindi
    in fields of mountain flowers and loco weed,

peace huddled under army surplus blankets
    on haiku hillsides,

big busted broad bottomed hippie girls
    with hirsute mystic armpits and moonshot eden eyes

sprouted in enchanted woods, cooing mantras,
    simmering potions, humming the wind,

danced without music, naked and spicy
    under tie-dyed peasant skirts,

hunted lost goddesses behind
    no trespassing signs on deserted farms.

A pill on their tongues,
    indian bracelets jangling,

they led us barefoot into new gardens
    on the other side of the interstate,

yes on their lips, yes to everything,
    marking the places we shared the universal Ah

with tattooed cosmic signs,
    smiling even as we stumbled away,

having no clue the glad gifts
    they sprinkled over us in acid bright midnights

would be squandered so recklessly,
    no premonition the long stemmed buds

they scattered along the unforgiving streets
    would burst into candleflame, blossom into fists.

Getting Older

Sometimes what you remember is their voices again,
coming on inside you like strung lights in your blood,
certain words they'd tongue differently
from anyone else, or your own name
and its surprisingly infinite nuances.
And sometimes you remember their hands,
not touching you but draped over a steering wheel
or cupped briefly around a cigarette,
anywhere you could watch them
in their life apart from you, knowing how
they'd find you later, blind but sure,
and come to rest where you needed them.
You remember the hardness of their bellies,
the soft line of hair that swirls down
toward the cock, the look of each one
that entered you and then withdrew, or lay
quietly inside awhile longer before slipping
away like a girl sneaking out in the middle
of the night, high heels dangling from one hand
as her stockinged feet drew sparks from the rug.
Sometimes you wander the house all day,
the fog outside stalled at the tops
of trees, refusing to rise higher and reveal
the world you hope is still there, the one
in which you're still a woman
some beautiful man might helplessly
move toward. And you remember how one
looked at you the first time you undressed,
how another didn't mind that you cried.
Sometimes it's enough just to say
their names like a rosary, ordinary names
linked by nothing but the fact
that they belong to men who loved you. And finally
you depend on that, you pray it's enough
to last, if it has to, the rest of your life.

Scan

Near the heart lies the cupboard
into which I carefully filed the ruined breast of my grandmother
then removed it
& her pale blue jars of threads & buttons

In the belly
the angry letters I stitched to the doorways & mountains of Phu Bai
for the 13 months my brother risked everything

Husks of planter's warts removed without painkiller dot the right heel
Cinder fragments from the bad bike accident the left

Lost constellations inside my uterus still glow
for the tissues torn out
My spirit swims and flies there alongside

the pulsing dome of my mother's lost ovary
her mother's 10 pregnancies & 10 homebed deliveries

Veils of my father's insomnia wrap the skull's frontal
interiors so that dreaming wide-awake comes naturally

The hairline crack at the base of the spine
from the summer party I slid, stoned, down a dozen steps

curls like a serpent of wandering intent
its fire another tongue of irretrievable speech

Everywhere the microscopic lines
left by skin on skin, the oceanic & moraine-
kissed traces of lovers

Under the right ribcage are the wild red foxes
I found in a beautiful dream
In bluegray mist where they run
it's always morning, when breathing is easiest

and I awaken
refreshed, restored to this body
this house I carry alone

Outliving Our Ghosts

—for Al Miller

You show me the X ray,
tell me how the bullet clipped the rim of your helmet,
sheared off the top of your ear,
continued downward into the shoulder
where the nerves cable under the collarbone,
soft as the white of an eye, and there,
broke up and stopped. The Jews say,
Bad times past are good to tell of.
Al, did we dream it all?
With your fingers you trace bullet fragments,
how they have moved over the years
as your body continued its path toward the death
that touched your shoulder twenty years ago
and spun you back into life with your eyes open.
Flesh alive then is no longer part of us.
If each cell is new every seven years,
what is the heart's tattoo?
And the years between. You finding Buddha
in a young Vietnamese you killed;
me getting sober, seeing my life stand up
as from the tall grass,
where it had lain all this time, covered with signs.
Talking again we honor the darkness,
breathe again the sweet air of a second life.
We are here and we are whole.
I hold the X ray up to the light:
the fragments still in your flesh,
bright winter stars.

The Art of Comedy

Comedy naturally wears itself out.
—*Hazlitt*

 Girded, half-conscious
 from incredible drugs, I lay in bed
like a tuber—I can
 say this now—I lay stretched white
 and groaning, girdled

 tightly from nipples to
 crotch so as not to rip my unstitched,
stapled, sliced-apart
 belly apart. I floated. I cast about
 my dim bulb for retorts

 to the nurses begging me
 to pee, to jump-start my hours' dead kidneys,
and couldn't give them
 a drop, nozzled as I was to a bent-
 neck plastic bottle.

 They dribbled water in the sink
 and giggled. They whispered threats of
catheter, the big orderly,
 as I drifted in the backwash
 of drugs and IVs

 under blue of the afternoon movies—
Clousseau fighting a doomsday device while
Dreyfuss goes slobbering mad,
 Barney slitting the Mayberry air
 with karate's

 keen self-importance,
 till Andy shrugs at Aunt Bea—
all the hyperbolic,
 needle-sharp comics come to haunt me
 with their menacing laughter, enemy

to a cut-open abdomen.
Nurses kept tabs on my pulse rate. Abbott aped
at Costello, and someone
said *urine*. Nothing. Dreyfuss stumbled,
sputtered, foiled again.

Then, *How are we feeling?*
And all the pent-up silliness began to gurgle
in my belly, *don't*
laugh, and the still-spastic muscles quivered
and I giggled with pain, *watch it,*

careful! but too late: I cut loose
laughing, my hydraulic bed shook,
the nurses bit back
their sympathetic snickers,
and just like that

I was weeping,
racked out in unspeakable hurt,
choking on sobs
between gasping and hoots. They held me down
and shot me up, stern-faced angels

armed with pity, blankets
—their tragic equipment—checked and checked
my pressure, all comedy
shoved aside for the headliner, pain, slicking
its hair and lighting up.

The Rapture

I remember standing in the kitchen, stirring bones for soup,
and in that moment, I became another person.

It was an early spring evening, the air California mild.
Outside, the eucalyptus was bowing compulsively

over the neighbor's motor home parked in the driveway.
The street was quiet for once, and all the windows were open.

Then my right arm tingled, a flutter started under the skin.
Fire charged down the nerve of my leg; my scalp exploded

in pricks of light. I shuddered and felt like laughing;
it was exhilarating as an earthquake. A city on fire

after an earthquake. Then I trembled and my legs shook,
and every muscle gripped so I fell and lay on my side,

a bolt driven down my skull into my spine. My legs were
swimming against the linoleum, and I looked up at the underside

of the stove, the dirty places where the sponge didn't reach.
Everything collapsed there in one place, one flash of time.

There in my body. In the kitchen at six in the evening, April.
A wooden spoon clutched in my hand, the smell of chicken broth.

And in that moment I knew everything that would come after:
the vision was complete as it seized me. Without diagnosis,

without history, I knew that my life was changed.
I seemed to have become entirely myself in that instant.

Not the tests, examinations in specialists' offices, not
the laboratory procedures: MRI, lumbar puncture, electrodes

pasted to my scalp, the needle scraped along the sole of my foot,
following one finger with the eyes, EEG, CAT scan, myelogram.

Not the falling down or the blindness and tremors, the stumble
and hiss in the blood, not the lying in bed in the afternoons.

Not phenobarbital, amitriptyline, prednisone, amantadine, ACTH,
cortisone, cytoxan, copolymer, baclofen, tegretol, but this:

Six o'clock in the evening in April, stirring bones for soup.
An event whose knowledge arrived whole, its meaning taking years

to open, to seem a destiny. It lasted thirty seconds, no more.
Then my muscles unlocked, the surge and shaking left my body

and I lay still beneath the white high ceiling. Then I got up
and stood there, quiet, alone, just beginning to be afraid.

Chemo

The nurse comes in to say
your potassium's low, so you mug
mock horror to make us laugh.
She hooks a vial to your IV:
This may burn.
Visiting hours, we're a bunch of lieutenants
with the jitters.
You try to keep the ball rolling.
My tongue curls in my head.
All right, I'll worry about the trees
instead. Some road crew's snipped the limbs
that would have dragged ice across the wires,
thinking it was safe and cold,
too late now, pruning in December.
The sun's alive behind its glaze.
Along the street the foolish sap pearls
and drips. It fills the tiny sidewalk craters,
runs in rivered cul-de-sacs, dries the same stain
of sugar kids splash on the driveways
eating watermelon in summer.
You're thinner than I ever remember.
Like a man judging fruit for heft,
you curve your hands around your calf,
weighing memory against flesh,
this body you live in differently,
a cellar step that can't be trusted.
You show me a track from last rib past navel,
the long seam women once opened
when doctors went in gangbusters after babies,
singing, give us this little one,
this feather, this fat olive.
From you they plucked, and sewed
and said, not enough.
I follow the stories forming in your eyes.

Give us some sweet, the needles cry,
take this slivered glass, these blood
spiders, these poisoned squeezings,
we have such thirst,
please oh please, take it.

Caribbean Breast Lullaby

—for L.S. and D.G. and others

Take it, now, while the sun is still
a pink shell on the horizon, while the cat
is still curled up at the foot of the bed,
while my husband is still in love with me.

Take it before it's too late to take it,
scrubbed clean of powders, colognes, body oils,
these last glittery grains of sand, the promiscuous
taste of rum and sea salt, before I can no longer

picture it as a rotting coconut weighing
my lifeboat down, a woody nest of termites,
a sack of moldy coriander seed, a milky
jellyfish ready to sting. How many men

have touched it I can keep counting like palm
fronds fanning the pale women in my own
motherline until I finally fall asleep below
the surgeon's knife. So go ahead.

Throw it overboard. It's had a full life.
Gone braless beneath the Indian silk shirts
of an exotic adolescence, awaited the mango
kisses of a calypso boy my parents forbid

me to let inside the house. At the ripe edge of
middle age now I'm ready. Let it return
underwater where it has always been most at home,
find the shortest way from Lake Michigan back

to Trinidad, resurface among fallen
ginger lilies and flying fish in that warm lagoon,
flamboyantly as an Empress Butterfly's
sapphirine wings, vanish before I change my mind.

Ashes

My left hand joggled Johnny's arm, and Johnny
—Jesus!—
          Johnny dropped the coffee can
holding his sister. The can
                 rolled jerkily,
the lid
        spun off, and Sister Rachel spilled
across the black linoleum.
Did I mention we'd been drinking? Everyone
stepped back,
          then back again.
                 Who wants
to track a woman's ashes on the floor
of a rented hall, then get home
             slightly drunk,
pull off his dress shoes and find a residue
of fine dust
        trapped in the polished leather creases,
especially if it's dust
          you know by name
and flirted with
           ungracefully a time or two:
"Nice shoes. I love those
           strap sandals." Rachel Fuller.
A few
      drunk mourners gasped, a few
              more giggled,
and since I was the one who knocked her loose
I rooted in the kitchen,
          found a broom,
but Johnny
        wrestled the splayed broom from my hands
and slapped the heavy ash and particles
of crushed bone toward the can.
            "Come on now, Rachel,"
he said, "you
        wild woman you," and weeping,

Johnny stabbed and swatted at the floor
until I found a paper towel,
                        wet it,
and mopped
            the last fine dust.
                        But what next?
At home I left it on the dresser. A month.
Three months.
            "Throw that revolting thing away!"
my wife said.
            Six months.
                        "Why are you keeping it?"
Rachel Fuller. Old possibility.
A little loud.
            Sharp. Quick.
                        A little sexy.
But what do I know? I met her at a party,
admired her taut,
            tan calves,
                        but praised her shoes,
and thought
            she might have been a little sorry
I couldn't find the sly
            next words to say.
Eight months her ashes challenged me to grieve.
But I kept waiting
            and, as I knew it would,
the magic
            leached away, the awe
                        withdrew,
and I disposed of it, her dust, as we do
almost all
            the dead—even those
                        we loved,
loved utterly—
            because they are sheer dust
and should be honored as the dust they are.

What the Living Do

Johnny, the kitchen sink has been clogged for days, some utensil
   probably fell down there.
And the Drano won't work but smells dangerous, and the crusty
   dishes have piled up

waiting for the plumber I still haven't called. This is the everyday
   we spoke of.
It's winter again: the sky's a deep headstrong blue, and the sunlight
   pours through

the open living room windows because the heat's on too high in
   here, and I can't turn it off.
For weeks now, driving, or dropping a bag of groceries in the street,
   the bag breaking,

I've been thinking: This is what the living do. And yesterday,
   hurrying along those
wobbly bricks in the Cambridge sidewalk, spilling my coffee down
   my wrist and sleeve,

I thought it again, and again later, when buying a hairbrush: This
   is it.
Parking. Slamming the car door shut in the cold. What you called
   that yearning.

What you finally gave up. We want the spring to come and the winter
   to pass. We want
whoever to call or not call, a letter, a kiss—we want more and more
   and then more of it.

But there are moments, walking, when I catch a glimpse of myself
   in the window glass,
say, the window of the corner video store, and I'm gripped by a
   cherishing so deep

for my own blowing hair, chapped face, and unbuttoned coat that
   I'm speechless:
I am living, I remember you.

Heroin

Imagine spring's thaw, your brother said,
each house a small rain, the eaves muttering
like rivers and you the white skin
the world sheds, your flesh unfolded

and absorbed. You walked Newark together,
tie loosened, a silk rainbow undone,
his fatigues the flat green of summer's end,
all blood drained from the horizon.

It would have been easier had you music
to discuss, a common love for one
of the brutal sports, if you shared
his faith that breath and sumac are more

alike than distinct, mutations of the same
tenacity. You almost tried it for him,
cinched a belt around your arm, aimed
a needle at the bloated vein, your window

open to July's gaunt wind and the radio
dispersing its chatty somnolence. When
he grabbed your wrist, his rightful face
came back for a moment: he was fifteen

and standing above Albert Ramos, fists
clenched, telling the boy in a voice
from the Old Testament what he'd do if certain
cruelties happened again. Loosening the belt,

you walked out, each straight and shaking,
into the hammering sun, talked of the past
as if it were a painting of a harvested field,
two men leaning against dusk and pitchforks.

That night he curled up and began to die,
his body a pile of ants and you on the floor
ripping magazines into a mound of words
and faces, touching his forehead with the back

of your hand in a ritual of distress, fading
into the crickets' metered hallucination.
When in two days he was human again, when
his eyes registered the scriptures of light,

when he tried to stand but fell and tried
again, you were proud but immediately
began counting days, began thinking
his name were written in a book

locked in the safe of a sunken ship,
a sound belonging to water, to history,
and let him go, relinquished him
to the strenuous work of vanishing.

Are You Experienced?

While Jimi Hendrix played "Purple Haze" onstage,
scaling his guitar like a black cat
up a high-voltage, psychedelic fence,

I was in the parking lot of the rock festival,
trying to get away from the noise and
looking for my car because

I wanted to have something familiar
to throw up next to. The haze I was in
was actually ultraviolet, the murky lavender

of the pills I had swallowed
several hundred years before,
pills that had answered so many of my questions,

they might as well have been guided tours
of miniature castles and museums,
microscopic Sistine Chapels

with room for everyone inside.
—But now something was backfiring,
and I was out on the perimeter of history,

gagging at the volume of raw data,
unable to recall the kind and color
of the car I owned,

and unable to guess, as I studied
the fresco of vomit on concrete,
that one day this moment

cleaned up and polished
would itself become
a kind of credential.

Drunk

What's the drunkest you've ever been,
he's asking. *Tell me.*
As if I've forgotten the perfect stillness
when my head fills with a luscious
rising, each new drink a pink
orbit around my head. I swallow it all.
Blackouts, I say, remembering
what it's like to step so far outside
that the body still continues. *Once
I drank a fifth of whiskey on a bet.* Eighteen
and aching, almost a rock
and roll death, a tangle of dried vomit
in my hair. I woke up. *A man
gave me a gun in a bar,* and I sat on it, hiding
the metal lump under the thick spread
of my thighs. It pinched. *I left eggs
boiling on the stove,* wandered home hours later
to their lovely moist explosions,
all the water fizzed away. Vanished. Their hard
little shells were dead white scraps littering
the kitchen counters. *Had sex with a stranger
at a party.* I left him there, on the shower stall floor
when it was over, unconscious and dribbling
into the drain. *Stole three thousand cocktail swords
from a bar's closet,* my coat pocket stuffed
with their unsettled sharpness, then I tossed them
in someone's yard. *I threw up
on a woman's shoe.* My lover's mother didn't seem
surprised. She washed her foot, mopped
the floor and my pale face, put me back to bed.
Drunk enough to meet you,
I tell him, remembering our walk home through
the woods, staggering over snow
packed hard enough to hold us up. We roll
over in the cold dark, dizzy,
dizzy with what? *Drunk enough for you,* I say.

Loudmouth Soup

Vodka, whisky, gin. Scotch. Red wine, cognac,
brandy—are you getting thirsty yet?—ale,
rye. It all tastes good: on the rocks, with a splash,
side of soda, shaken
not stirred, triple
olives, one of those nutritious little pearl
onions, a double, neat,
with a twist. Drink
it up, let's have *a* drink: dry beer, wet beer,
light, dark, and needled beer. Oh parched,
we drank the river
nearly to its bed at times, and were so numb
a boulder on a toe
was pleasant pain, all pain
was pleasant since that's all there was, pain,
and everything that was deeply felt, deeply,
was not. Bourbon, white and pink wine, *apéritif*,
cordial (hardly!), cocktail, martini,
highball, *digestif*, port, grain
punch—are you getting thirsty yet?—line them up!
We'll have *a* drink
and talk, we'll have
a drink and sleep, we'll
have *a* drink
and die, grim-about-it-with-piquancy.
It was a long time on the waiting list
for zero
and I'm happy
for the call out of that line
to other, less predictable,
more joyful
slides to ride on home.

After Detox

I

"For ten days panic will claw your face, then it will be over."

I like the pale light best: the light of dusk
and the light of dawn. And in the hours between—the soft
yellow in the light of closed eyes. On my back,
sometimes I clench them for flashes—like worrying
the red dictionary for words—that don't cut
deep enough. My arms have finally released
my body. My body has fallen back into itself,
fallen into an undisturbed place where nerves
lead nowhere. I think—life. I think—death.
Laundry, I think. Eat. Laundry. Death. Eat.
The light comes softly around curtains; the light
leaves slowly, leaking out around curtains. The sun
is rising and falling. No dying claims my thoughts;
no gem of whisky, no flower of opium
names them. I do my laundry every evening,
walk mechanically down the faded street to where the warm
machines rattle and hum, and the warm soap splashes
behind glass. A life as clean as a bed.
A bed in a room. My hand goes out to touch
a teacup. It is there. Nothing moves in the pure
dim behind my eyes, where thoughts once darted. I wait.
My socks will match. My hair will shine. I like
the pale light best. The light of dusk and the light of dawn.
It seeps around my life slowly. It leaves
without knocking. It has no ending and no beginning,
and all the rest—that other death they call living.

II

"Living"

Everybody in my family has something he must do
to hold us all up; two days after my mother
took me home I had my old job back. I work

at a diner. Luci's Place—with a lot of road traffic
and some regulars. Luci's Place—with sunflowers
between the parking lot and the light green
concrete-block wall; in summer their stems bend
under the huge weight of blossoms. I hide
under grubby clatter; I work at a diner
on the outskirts of town, but it's the green glare
of trees—which hurts my eyes—I died for.

In the morning, sitting in my nightgown by the window,
I watch the light seep around the corners of Glen's Garage.
Yellow, orange, blue. Colors of the rainbow
or the sky rising. Colors on the rusted plates
on the rusted cars. Cars with their toes turned up,
tires sold, fenders missing. Cars from all over, with maps
of stars on the windshields where heads have smashed.

I read stories full of people with descriptions—
some of them have noses that are big, eyes that are small,
skin that is bad, but noses, eyes and skin somebody
has bothered to describe. I try to think of my life in plot.
Bamboozled. But I laugh, for I know that the sunflowers
and the old cars with the pale light at their edges
are all the beauty I'll ever need to hold me up.

I speak softly to the light when its white hands
warm my cheeks. I speak softly to the world,
but I can never explain the way life fades
as it approaches, the way, mid-sentence, I'll realize
it's not me who is speaking, and listen
to the strange words of a strange voice. Or the way
what it is that I'm meant to be doing is always
just on the tip of my tongue. Or why I began
in the northwest quadrant of my forehead,
just above the hairline, and carved, with mother's
dullest knife, the long diagonal line that ends
at the right side of my jaw. Or how the wide red scar

—its shiny translucent skin—turned out
exactly as I wanted. I can never explain,
but it should speak for itself—the map
of a vision, proof that I exist. It's only honest—
to wear your skin as if it were your own.

February

—*for Michael Van Walleghen*

Snow falls upon snow. It piles up on the roads, mile after gray mile
of it catches in the wheelwells of the car. It piles up like debt, like
failure, and, as your mother pointed out, you've put on a few pounds
since Christmas. Now in February the winter seems permanent,
glacial. Each snowfall is more a feeling than an external event, a
heaviness, shortness of breath. . . . You wake in a panic, tearing at
the blankets. . . . It's only a cat. A large house cat. You've wakened
in an overheated room in a strange house with the family cat
sleeping on your chest. You are a guest, you don't belong here.
Heart pounding, you want to be on your way. But it's the middle of
the night, in winter. There's no place to go. . . . You won't be here
very long. Relax. Nothing has changed. You are who you've always
been, only more so.

Late Summer News

Applications are now being accepted for public burning.
—Radio announcement, Charlotte, N.C.

Come over here from over there, girl.
—Bob Dylan, "Don't Fall Apart on Me Tonight"

Up and down this red clay route
where heat makes waves, mailboxes
hold a stiff salute above the chokeweed:
today, against all odds,
someone has remembered you.
My hand tests the little oven.
Visa, J. C. Penney, Southern Bell, these mornings I confess
I'm happy to find bills there
or anything bearing my name
plain as light through a wax paper window.
"Pledge to the Radical Gay Alliance,"
"Plant a Tree in Israel,"
even the stacked deck of other people's needs
I read lovingly. Then this:
an envelope, flatbread and salt,
from a friend who writes for nothing I can give.
J & L Steel turns the air orange, she says,
in the old neighborhood.
Bag ladies shamble up and down Murray Avenue,
still speaking to the personal angels
who live in their coat pockets,
and caged live chickens
bask in Neederman's doorway, waiting to be delivered
unto the butcher and the rabbi.
"What I mean most is that laughter
won't be the same without you."
Her daughter, she closes, has grown gorgeous
and last month married for love.

Who knows what to wish for?
The big picture hides in its own wide margins—
no one sees it or why
we sign our names to each day that comes
wearing its New Wave fashions.
But when the white parachute of faith or memory blooms
backward from this letter in my hand,
I'm ready for it, am meant to see
projected in its pure, billowing center
how the blind really do lead us.
There, my father in his catcher's squat in 1946,
a Tareyton dangling from his lips—
his slow, loopy charm.
My mother at Sacred Heart High
taking lessons in resisting charm, fingers crossed.
My Italian grandfather kneeling
to his 80th garden, basil, fennel, chard;
my Irish grandfather's cancer
thriving like a wrung note in his vocal chords.
Friends, I see them, too,
playing air guitars and clinking bottles of Iron City
against Mouton Rothschild, 1976.
If choices were wood
I could build a bridge back to them
with the choices I've made to be here.
I could burn one down.
This morning, head tilted, I think
I must look for all the world
like that RCA dog, full of dopey trust and waiting.
The gravel makes a noise under my feet
like just-thrown dice, and
what silk there is floats away from me
over hundred-year pines,
all the bright strings attached.

Antilamentation

Regret nothing. Not the cruel novels you read
to the end just to find out who killed the cook.
Not the insipid movies that made you cry in the dark,
in spite of your intelligence, your sophistication.
Not the lover you left quivering in a hotel parking lot,
the one you beat to the punchline, the door, or the one
who left you in your red dress and shoes, the ones
that crimped your toes, don't regret those.
Not the nights you called god names and cursed
your mother, sunk like a dog in the livingroom couch,
chewing your nails and crushed by loneliness.
You were meant to inhale those smoky nights
over a bottle of flat beer, to sweep stuck onion rings
across the dirty restaurant floor, to wear the frayed
coat with its loose buttons, its pockets full of struck matches.
You've walked those streets a thousand times and still
you end up here. Regret none of it, not one
of the wasted days you wanted to know nothing,
when the lights from the carnival rides
were the only stars you believed in, loving them
for their uselessness, not wanting to be saved.
You've traveled this far on the back of every mistake,
ridden in dark-eyed and morose but calm as a house
after the TV set has been pitched out the upstairs
window. Harmless as a broken ax. Emptied
of expectation. Relax. Don't bother remembering
any of it. Let's stop here, under the lit sign
on the corner, and watch all the people walk by.

These Are My Buddhist Shoes

They are lined with juniper-berry
breath & finch-head purple
velvet. Their three-inch wood soles
make me practice mindfulness
with every step: rightleftrightright. Left.
Oh, I have suffered in these shoes.
Oh, I have been holy in these shoes,
and I have also not been.
When the world says rush,
I wear these shoes. Look,
the strap is embroidered
with hummingbird feathers &
high-mass red flowers,
a certain goofball every time
my foot steps down. These shoes
give what Lourdes promises.
These are the improbable shoes
of my 50s. In case you didn't notice
they are sturdy & quite beautiful.

Memory as a Hearing Aid

Somewhere, someone is asking a question,
and I stand squinting at the classroom
with one hand cupped behind my ear,
trying to figure out where that voice is coming from.

I might be already an old man,
attempting to recall the night
his hearing got misplaced,
front-row-center at a battle of the bands,

where a lot of leather-clad, second-rate musicians,
amped up to dinosaur proportions,
test drove their equipment through our ears.
Each time the drummer threw a tantrum,

the guitarist whirled and sprayed us with machine-gun riffs,
as if they wished that they could knock us
quite literally dead.
We called that fun in 1970,

when we weren't sure our lives were worth surviving.
I'm here to tell you that they were,
and many of us did, despite ourselves,
though the road from there to here

is paved with dead brain cells,
parents shocked to silence,
and squad cars painting the whole neighborhood
the quaking tint and texture of red jelly.

Friends, we should have postmarks on our foreheads
to show where we have been;
we should have pointed ears, or polka-dotted skin
to show what we were thinking

when we hot-rodded over God's front lawn,
and Death kept blinking.
But here I stand, an average-looking man
staring at a room

where someone blond in braids
with a beautiful belief in answers
is still asking questions.

Through the silence in my dead ear,
I can almost hear the future whisper
to the past: it says that this is not a test
and everybody passes.

VI

WHY THE DOG HOWLS AT THE MOON

The Owl and the Lightning

—Brooklyn, New York

No pets in the projects,
the lease said,
and the contraband salamanders
shriveled on my pillow overnight.
I remember a Siamese cat, surefooted
I was told, who slipped from a window ledge
and became a red bundle
bulging in the arms of a janitor.

This was the law on the night
the owl was arrested.
He landed on the top floor,
through the open window
of apartment 14-E across the hall,
a solemn white bird bending the curtain rod.
In the cackling glow of the television,
his head swiveled, his eyes black.
The cops were called, and threw a horse blanket
over the owl, a bundle kicking.

Soon after, lightning jabbed the building,
hit apartment 14-E, scattering bricks from the roof
like beads from a broken necklace.
The sky blasted white, detonation of thunder.
Ten years old at the window, I knew then that God
was not the man in my mother's holy magazines,
touching fingertips to dying foreheads
with the half-smile of an athlete signing autographs.
God must be an owl, electricity
coursing through the hollow bones,
a white wing brushing the building.

Lourdes

Where be all his miracles
which our fathers told us of?
—Judges 6:13

There were rumors:
if the men took pay cuts,
gave up sick time and vacations,

shaved some insurance benefits,
our mill might be spared.
We waited for a sign.

The blessed mother did not appear
on the project playground,
and when Mrs. Cavelli cut her palm

slicing pepperoni, Father Conko shook
his head, said that wasn't really *stigmata.*
Round the clock women in babushkas

prayed the rosary. Candles burned
in rows at St. Michael's and St. Joe's.
All that smoke and incense,

still, not one statue wept.
At the union hall, some of the men
came drunk, cursing. My father (who never

spoke before a crowd) stood up:
Don't give the sonsabitches nothing back,
we worked too damn hard to get what we have.

Let the bastards close her down.
We waited for a sign.
The next day they hung it on the gate.

Viceroy

My mother used to lock me out of the house
when she'd had enough of my shenanigans.
I'd have to pry the screen open
with a screwdriver to get my body back inside.
I'd stand out there strategizing, breathing the cool air.
I could see the fire of her cigarette intensify
when she took a drag, there inside her dark
bedroom, shade partly lifted, watching me.
The outside air was full of heavy yellow smoke
from the burn barrels, the paper mill, mushroom
factory, leaf burning. Hungry, I'd crave a potato
roasted in some roaring pile of leaves guarded by
a big sensible father. I leaned up against the oak tree
which had been split right in half by a lightning bolt,
open as a boy's unzipped fly.
It seemed like *open* always meant I was caught
in the cop's headlights in the vineyard
and somebody's pants were down.

Do you see, God, how I do not want to have to die
to get to come home? Being your child,
I want to be so alive that you gasp when I arrive.
You acknowledge the grape juice on my lips.
You light your Viceroy on the sparks in my hair.

Why the Dog Howls at the Moon

Because it is round, and too large to be swallowed up whole
or to be nudged along the ground; because it is too far away

for her to take huge snapping bites of it; because once her head
is tilted back, sound rolls up great wallops of noise

that bounce from all of her delicate acoustic teeth until each note
rounds itself into an orb, a golden sphere of waves and particles,

ready to tumble across the night in its asteroid-pocked perfection.
Because it is yellow, and she is beyond shouting; because joy

and despair are too large to be held in a small sound,
a small body, a small rock hurtling through space.

Because her heart is broken and comes up from her chest in pieces
that rattle and moan in her throat; because there is no one

to pat her back, to rub her head and sides, to tell her it will one night
be over, that what she will have left after the howling

is the memory of pain and not this musical agony;
because the night demands some sacrifice and she has made it

unselfishly, with her long dog-snout and her great dog-lungs
and her heart, which we all thought unbreakable.

Not Believing

I.

    Faith is a car, my student says, driven
    on wheels of facts. What facts, I ask. We have

    talked of wars, famine, centuries of
    genocide. The Old Testament prophesies,

    he argues, are fulfilled in the Christ's coming—
    a fact proven by Gospel. Smiling, he

    pulls a card from his wallet about
    Wednesday night Bible studies in his

    dorm room. You think faith is a leap, he says,
    off the Grand Canyon. But if you follow

    the facts logically, you will walk right
    into it, you will bump your head against

    it and laugh. I don't think I'll be laughing,
    I say, accepting the card. He frowns the way

    good people frown when unsure of insults,
    then says, Maybe we'll see you there. If

    he were not my student, he would lift his
    hand; he would lay it on my shoulder in

    the comradely-consoling manner of pastors.

II.

    I used to take communion
    of grape juice in
    doll's cups, white
    bread cut into cubes
    like the handful my mother

scattered on the balcony
for sparrows. In Sunday School,
a pink cloud of swine stuck itself
on the flannel board beside
the Prodigal Son—the fact
of his hunger clarified
by black pellets we bought at
zoos to feed the ducks, the otters:
when famine came, he ate pigs'
food. There were sleep-overs
in summer to learn Bible
verses and the apostles'
journeys, and at Christmas,
my younger brother in a striped
bedsheet worshipping a baby
doll, with everyone on
the stage in night gowns and
sheets as though the miracle,
too, were a sleep-over of
sorts. I believed one Easter
at sunrise when the pastor
described the disciples roasting
fish over their small fires on
the shore. I imagined them
squinting into the fish-blue smoke
the way my grandparents might
have, when the Lord appeared,
His live fingers eager to
tear bread, to touch.

III.

I do not wish to walk into belief
as if into a basement with a cheap

flashlight, feeling my way in slippers,

knocking over Salvation Army clothes, a rusted

dehumidifier. If I wanted, still,
to believe, I would leap off the canyon

wall into the green smoke of sage or
juniper and fall toward desert fires

at once familiar and mysterious—
constellations whose names

we have forgotten.

If There Is No God

Then there's no one
to love us indiscriminately,
to twirl our planet like a globe, to keep the sap—
xylem and phloem—gliding up and down like the slide
of a trombone, the cells breathing through teeming mitochondria,
slurping rain, eating sunlight.

The jawless lamprey clamps its round
mouth on the flank of a fish, rasping and sucking blood.
The hinged-jaw python ingests a velvet-cloaked gazelle.

Spider silk, the polypeptide chain folded
back and forth, pleated sheets stronger than steel.
They stretch and coil, responding like a lover.
Who will notice? Who will watch
while the articulate legs wrap the dragonfly
round and round, huge wings whirring?

Who will crouch beside the lichen as it wheedles into rock,
mark its single millimeter's growth like a father penciling tracks
up the back of the door? And when it dies—
a thousand, two thousand years old, this modest
leaflike, shrublike creature, poisoned,
who will mourn? Who will chant its elegy?

The polar ice caps are cracking up.
The people of whole continents collapsing—viruses bud
continuously from the graceful, convoluted surfaces of T cells,
gathering and heaping in intricate curls and valleys.
We cannot find a single ivory-billed woodpecker or Tasmanian wolf.
Radioactive fallout circles the planet.

There must be something you love: the cherry trees
on Storrow Drive bursting into bloom as you pass,
each tree releasing its pale buds like pastel fireworks.
Or driving back from Poipu Beach, the children slumped against you,
the moon flashing through the thousand palms.

When finches go crazy gorging and singing
in the last of the November pears, when Pavarotti sings,
or a mother sings to her baby, "I can't give you anything but love,"
walking the stained carpet of the hallway,
when she falls back into bed and her new lover gathers
her up like a honeycomb, someone
must pay attention. Open your window.
Listen, listen to them, and behold.

We Were Simply Talking

We were simply talking, probably work, or relatives
or even Christmas presents, when the car slid
and I corrected, fishtailed and I corrected, then we were gone,
sliding sideways, sliding backward on black ice
and staring into the grill of a diesel tractor, also sliding,
and in that instant I was ready to die.
I saw my wife and was overjoyed that I had married her,
though our marriage was already falling apart,
and I loved the car, a brown Toyota, loved
being warm in the car while it was white, cold, bitter
out in the world we'd lost control of. I loved
every molecule of breath I wasn't taking,
and for the moment I forgave myself every sin
and failure of my life, including this
ridiculous and undignified early death.
The car snapped backward into a frozen ditch.
I sat speechless, shaking, my wife speechless also,
and a man pulled up, a salesman: You folks okay?
Suddenly the radio roared, and by the car
a dog barked wildly and, yes, we were fine.
Fine. We were fine. But what was "fine," I wondered,
and why do we always, always have to speak?

A Long Commute

Faith is a long commute. Lots
of time to change
the station on the radio, time
to relive the past, to consider

the future the way
the boy in the bus station
standing by the trashcan
the afternoon the bomb went off
must have had time to consider

his own hands carefully in his hands. The road

is narrow and it goes

straight through the gardens of Paradise. Lots

of soggy godhearts dripping
blood on their bloody vines. Behind me

a beautiful blind girl carries a Bible
home in a plastic bag, while

before me, an old
woman and her old mother
drive a Cadillac over
the flowers slowly.

Dennis's Sky Leopard

He saw it first, me just the big, the
little dippers and questions about
when they'd be full, ready to pour
something into me, anything, not just
what I've needed so long I've forgotten
what it is. He said

"I love him." How familiar
that sounded; I love him too, the one
steering the planets, a very male
thing to do; a woman admits to difficulty
in just navigating one small life, maneuvering
it away from diapers, last minute trips to Messina's
for bell peppers that don't chime, for both
angel and devil's food cake mixes to hide the truth,
for sugarless gum, sugarless colas and lemon limes,
ginger drinks full of pin pricks,

because the honeymoon is over; the grace period
is gone; the music must be faced now, rock lyrics
that slap with the full force of Rolling Stones,
verifying that you're the only sinner in the world.
Dennis said, "He's up in the air." I tried
to suck him up my nose. Dennis said, "He can't
come down." So he defies gravity, he breaks
bad laws, he's a male Antigone, a man I'd like
to meet if he weren't a leopard
and without domestic instincts like men.

This leopard takes up the whole sky, decorated
(as in purple, love-bruised hearts)
with constellations, star-quality spots.
He lives better up there than in the jungle.

Rain is an attempt at spot give-away. They melt.
Something about our atmosphere and hospitality.

I tilt my head, let it rain in my throat. Inside
I feel like a wheat field ready for perfect
harvest leading to ultimate feast but I'm never
cut down. That's the best part.

Mount Olive

Mount Olive Primitive Baptist Church is two miles from my home.
She is a calla lily growing in deep woods. On the third Sunday of
each month, I sit in the middle of the fourth pew beneath the jade
shower of the skylight. I join other ample women and our rail-thin
sisters in testimony and tears. The hymns are cradles and bayonets—
nesting our laments and pressing us on. We sing like we have known
each other all of our lives; our voices thickly woven ropes, making
ladders. Vaselined children with swinging feet draw on their legs
and rock to the rhythm. Thin brown men in thinning brown suits
punctuate the preacher's cadence with shouts and the percussion
of their canes and polished shoes. The faithful rise and fall in the
spirit like dolphin. Guardians in starched white uniforms resuscitate
the overwhelmed with gentle, gloved pats to powdered faces. The
elder women whisper underground words to call the faint back from
their peaceful homes. They wield their fans with the skill of a signal
corps. Elation evaporates from our bodies. Mercy rains down. Our
tongues capture the tonic and we are saved. The service ends with
hummingbirds calling "A-men" and the reverberation of small,
powerful wings. We drift out to our cars. Well-worn leather bibles
cross our hearts and touch the sky. The children pile into backseats
to watch the church disappear through dusty windshields; their
minds on early supper.

A Non-Christian on Sunday

Now we heathens have the town to ourselves.
We lie around, munching award-winning pickles
and hunks of coarse, seeded bread smeared
with soft, sweet cheese. The streets seem
deserted, as if Godzilla had been sighted
on the horizon, kicking down skyscrapers
and flattening cabs. Only two people
are lined up to see a popular movie
in which the good guy and the bad guy trade
faces. Churches burst into song. Trees wish
for a big wind. Burnt bacon and domestic tension
scent the air. So do whiffs of lawn mower exhaust
mixed with the colorless blood of clipped hedges.
For whatever's about to come crashing down
on our heads, be it bliss-filled or heinous,
make us grateful, OK? Hints of the savior's
flavor buzz on our tongues, like crumbs
of a sleeping pill shaped like a snowflake.

Refusing to Baptize a Son

Twilight came and my mother-in-law
Insisting again it would mean nothing,
The ceremony and the holy water,
And happiness of friends and family,
Which is everything to an old woman.
High tide at *el estero*, the Pacific roared

As beer turned to wine and wine to bourbon.
Midnight, fireworks, *Feliz Año Nuevo*,
And us, deep in our cups, and drinking on:
Me with my immutable gringo silence,
And her parrying, "What if he should die?"
And "You don't understand. You're not Roman."

What's changed now that she's buried?
Not nature, not my no, as dumb as yes,
Not the luck of the Spanish armada,
Or high muck I dreamed of defending:
Post-ethnic, post-religious, eclectic—
It's like her heaven. It doesn't exist.

Her spirit does. Stubborn. Procrustean. Loving
The palm tree's lovely freedom from knowledge.
May my son remember his grandmother
Alive in the tropics, standing for him,
Even in these words, even if they mark
The superstitions of an agnostic.

The Dashboard Virgencita

In César Chávez country, one of my young, white students wrote
an essay in which she criticized how local Mexican people put the
Virgin Mary on their dashboard. "It's in poor taste," she argued,
"not to mention kind of sacrilegious."

La Virgen on the dashboard is good taste
if you speak Spanish and believe in God.
Never mind the bumper stickers
or the nodding dog that agrees with everyone,
the showy vans on display on the highway
with seventy-miles-an-hour Salvador Dalis.
That's them, the white folks, who grew up in English
and believe driving is a practicing religion.
They've made their cars into false gods
and think the radio's revelation.
We know Who to thank when we get there.
We know just a couple of years ago
we would have required angels to move this fast.
With the help of our dashboard Virgencita
we'll keep up with them, pass them.
Maybe She'll raise one of her hands
and wave, jangle her dangling rosary
at them like a broken chain.
She'll think of something to teach them a lesson.
And we, we'll have good taste once we've eaten
the fruit of our cheap pickings in their Edens.

What Saves Us

We are wrapped around each other
in the back of my father's car parked
in the empty lot of the high school
of our failures, sweat on her neck
like oil. The next morning I would leave
for the war and I thought I had something
coming for that, I thought to myself
that I would not die never having
been inside her body. I lifted
her skirt above her waist like an umbrella
blown inside out by the storm. I pulled
her cotton panties up as high
as she could stand. I was on fire. Heaven
was in sight. We were drowning
on our tongues and I tried
to tear my pants off when she stopped
so suddenly we were surrounded
only by my shuddering
and by the school bells
grinding in the empty halls.
She reached to find something,
a silver crucifix on a silver chain,
the tiny savior's head
hanging, and stakes through his hands and his feet.
She put it around my neck and held me
so long my heart's black wings were calmed.
We are not always right
about what we think will save us.
I thought that dragging the angel down that night
would save me, but I carried the crucifix in my pocket
and rubbed it on my face and lips
nights the rockets roared in.
People die sometimes so near you,
you feel them struggling to cross over,
the deep untangling, of one body from another.

Fundamental

Acts of God,
the insurance people, whose business depends
on fear of them,
call them: hurricane, monsoon, cyclone,
whirlwind—when your house bears
the branches' lash, big winds
lift and slam the clapboards.
Little spiders, spirit receptors,
living in the walls or swinging
above the sills, sense it
first, are humble. The fiery,
the fundamental God
is mad, again. He gets that way,
decides to smash or flood
and it's no use to build a sandbag wall
around your acre, to try to divert
the torrents via channel
dug by hand. Or, He says: No water,
not a drop. I'll burn
their legumes to dust,
swell and crack their black black tongues.
Oh no—fire ants, weevil, mouse plague,
locusts: with a hundred neighbors
we'll beat the fields with rakes
and brooms—hopeless, hopeless—but our effort
saves a few more loaves
for winter—until God gives them mold: Cold *and*
hungry, He says. He says: These bugs
are tiny and bad,
mostly, I don't like their habits—so greedy,
mean, what'll shape them up
is fire and noise, their fields
I'll burn and barren,
what they need are heaps of pumice,
ash up to their ears,
and their sky, under my feet,
their sky, bloody and wracked, I'll split with howls.

The Mystery of Meteors

I am out before dawn, marching a small dog through a meager park
Boulevards angle away, newspapers fly around like blind white birds
Two days in a row I have not seen the meteors
though the radio news says they are overhead
Leonid's brimstones are barred by clouds; I cannot read
the signs in heaven, I cannot see night rendered into fire

And yet I do believe a net of glitter is above me
You would not think I still knew these things:
I get on the train, I buy the food, I sweep, discuss,
consider gloves or boots, and in the summer,
open windows, find beads to string with pearls
You would not think that I had survived
anything but the life you see me living now

In the darkness, the dog stops and sniffs the air
She has been alone, she has known danger,
and so now she watches for it always
and I agree, with the conviction of my mistakes.
But in the second part of my life, slowly, slowly,
I begin to counsel bravery Slowly, slowly,
I begin to feel the planets turning, and I am turning
toward the crackling shower of their sparks

These are the mysteries I could not approach when I was younger:
the boulevards, the meteors, the deep desires that split the sky
Walking down the paths of the cold park
I remember myself, the one who can wait out anything
So I caution the dog to go silently to bear with me
the burden of knowing what spins on and on above our heads

For this is our reward: Come Armageddon, come fire or flood,
come love, not love, millennia of portents—
there is a future in which the dog and I are laughing
Born into it, the mystery, I know we will be saved

Dear Earth

This is a love note from the sky: All
year I've watched you with my big eye, watched
the muscles in your back as I
stood behind you in the payroll line (those

muscles, are they roads, could they lead a woman into
the shadows of 5 o'clock
where she's always wanted to go?) I've

seen you in the parking lot
up to your knees in snow, scraping
the windshield of your white truck, which
spit a riddle of silver thumbtacks

into the silver night. When

you emerge from the Xerox room, I've
seen your conifers
tipped with light. I've

watched you sip
from the water cooler, too, tasting

its cool blue, seen
you pour your coffee
into styrofoam

until it overflowed.
And this I know:
The view

from here is too removed, diluted
as it is
with flirting & pollution. I want
to fall all over you like a farm, to bless

your fields with weeping, fists
of hail, black
feathers in a frenzy
out of their wrecked nests—simple

gracious rain on your white grapes, or

a holy blizzard of pain: My

tornadoes tearing up your prairies. My

red wind licking its initials in the dust.

Look

Your street at sundown.
Your window, the only one lit up

in all those apartments
stacked silhouette black

against the sky—what a color!
Like Sargasso—

loud, like they threw blue dye in it.
Citizen, look up,

the sky god is speaking.
Man, that blue is talking:

You on the old old earth,
listen to me, don't blast yourself.

There: the woman on your balcony.
The woman you let slip—

her forearms on the railing
letting the breeze mess with her sleeves.

Behind her in the room
the books unbend

hover off the shelves
and like a small space station

they wheel like electrons in her skirt—
the books open up to the lines you want

open like air
like water that opens wherever you already are.

Man, look up. Even a small child
has sense enough to drink that blue

whose beauty wounds him so precisely
he knows his life is worth saving.

Passing a Truck Full of Chickens
at Night on Highway Eighty

What struck me first was their panic.

Some were pulled by the wind from moving
to the ends of the stacked cages,
some had their heads blown through the bars—

and could not get them in again.
Some hung there like that—dead—
their own feathers blowing, clotting

in their faces. Then
I saw the one that made me slow some—
I lingered there beside her for five miles.

She had pushed her head through the space
between bars—to get a better view.
She had the look of a dog in the back

of a pickup, that eager look of a dog
who knows she's being taken along.
She craned her neck.

She looked around, watched me, then
strained to see over the car—strained
to see what happened beyond.

That is the chicken I want to be.

Kim Addonizio's most recent book, *Tell Me*, was nominated for the National Book Award in 2000. She is also the author of *The Philosopher's Club* and *Jimmy and Rita*; a book of stories entitled *In the Box Called Pleasure*; and the coauthor, with Dorianne Laux, of *The Poet's Companion: A Guide to the Pleasures of Writing Poetry*. Her many awards include fellowships from the National Endowment for the Arts.

Julia Alvarez's novels include *How the García Girls Lost Their Accents*, *In the Time of the Butterflies*, *Yo!*, and *In the Name of Salomé*. Books of poetry include *The Housekeeping Book*, *The Other Side/El Otro Lado*, and *Homecoming: New and Selected Poems*. *Something to Declare*, a book of essays, was published in 1998.

Doug Anderson is the author of three books of poetry, *Bamboo Bridge*, *The Moon Reflected Fire* (winner of the 1994 Kate Tufts Discovery Award), and *Blues for Unemployed Secret Police*. He has also written a play, *Short Times*, as well as critical essays, fiction, and film scripts.

Ginger Andrews's first book of poetry, *An Honest Answer*, won the Nicholas Roerich Poetry prize. She lives in Oregon, where she works cleaning houses and serving as a janitor and Sunday school teacher at North Bend Church of Christ.

David Baker's most recent of eight books are *Changeable Thunder* (poems) and *Heresy and the Ideal: On Contemporary Poetry* (criticism). He teaches at Denison University and in the MFA Program for Writers at Warren Wilson College. He also serves as poetry editor of the *Kenyon Review*.

Walter Bargen has published eight books of poetry, most recently *Harmonic Balance*. His poems have appeared in such magazines as the *Iowa Review*, *Boulevard*, and the *Beloit Poetry Journal*. He won the Chester H. Jones Foundation Poetry Prize in 1997.

Dorothy Barresi is the author of *Rouge Pulp*; *The Post-Rapture Diner*, winner of an American Book Award; and *All of the Above*, which won the Barnard New Women Poets Prize. Her honors include fellowships from the National Endowment for the Arts, the Fine Arts Work Center in Provincetown, and the North Carolina Arts Council, as well as a Pushcart Prize. She lives in Los Angeles and is a professor of English at California State University, Northridge.

Ellen Bass's most recent book of poetry is *Mules of Love*. She coedited the groundbreaking book *No More Masks! An Anthology of Poems by Women*, and her nonfiction books include *I Never Told Anyone*, *Free Your Mind*, and *The Courage to Heal*. Among her awards for poetry are the Elliston Book Award, the Pablo Neruda Prize, and the Larry Levis Prize.

Bill Bauer is the author of three books of poetry, including *Last Lambs*. His National Guard unit was activated during the race riots of 1968, and he was sent to Vietnam the following year. He is a cofounder and former president of Media/Professional Insurance, an international firm specializing in defending the first amendment rights of the media. He lives in Summit County, Colorado.

Robin Becker's most recent books are *All-American Girl*, winner of a Lambda Literary Award, and *The Horse Fair*. Her awards include fellowships from the National Endowment for the Arts and the Mary Bunting Institute of Radcliffe College. She teaches at Penn State University.

Erin Belieu's first book of poetry, *Infanta*, was a National Poetry Series winner. She is also the author of *One Above and One Below*. Belieu, the coeditor of *The Extraordinary Tide: New Poetry by American Women*, teaches creative writing at Ohio University in Athens.

Wendy Bishop divides her time between Alligator Point, Louisiana, and Tallahassee, Florida, where she is the Kellogg W. Hunt Distinguished Professor of English at Florida State University. Author of *Thirteen Ways of Looking for a Poem: A Guide to Writing Poetry* and *Reading into Writing: A Guide to Composing*, and editor of *The Writing Process Reader*, she has published several poetry chapbooks, including *Mid-Passage* and *Touching Liliana*. Her poems, stories, essays, and journals appear regularly in literary magazines and composition journals.

Bruce Bond's collections of poetry include *The Throats of Narcissus*, *Radiography*, and *The Anteroom of Paradise*. His poetry has appeared in the *Yale Review*, the *Paris Review*, the *New Republic*, the *Threepenny Review*, and many other journals, and his honors include fellowships from the National Endowment for the Arts and the Texas Commission on the Arts. He is a professor of English at the University of North Texas and poetry editor for the *American Literary Review*.

Philip Bryant is the author of *Sermon on a Perfect Spring Day* and the chapbook *Blue Island*. His work has appeared in journals such as the *Iowa Review*, the *Indiana Review*, and the *American Poetry Review*, and he has received a Minnesota State Arts Board Fellowship. He teaches at Gustavus Adolphus College.

Jeanne Bryner, a practicing registered nurse and teacher, is the author of two books of poetry, *Breathless* and *Tenderly Lift Me*. Her collection *Blind Horse* was published in 1999, and her new collection, *Eclipse*, is forthcoming in 2003.

Andrea Hollander Budy is the author of *House Without a Dreamer*, which won the Nicholas Roerich Poetry Prize, and *The Other Life*. Her awards include a D. H. Lawrence Fellowship from the University of New Mexico's Taos Summer Writers Conference, as well as fellowships from the National Endowment for the Arts and the Arkansas Arts Council.

Rick Campbell is the author of *A Day's Work* and *Setting the World in Order*, which won the 2000 Walt McDonald Prize in Poetry. His awards include a National Endowment for the Arts Fellowship and a Pushcart Prize. He teaches at Florida A&M University in Tallahassee and lives with his wife and daughter in Garden County, Florida. Since 1992, he has also served as Director of Anhinga Press and the Anhinga Prize for Poetry.

Nick Carbó is the author of *Secret Asian Man* and *El Grupo McDonald's*. He is also the editor of *Returning a Borrowed Tongue*, an anthology of Filipino and Filipino American Poetry, and coeditor of *Babaylan: An Anthology of Filipina and Filipina American Women's Writing*. His honors include grants from the National Endowment for the Arts and the New York Foundation for the Arts. His current project is *Sweet Jesus*, an anthology coedited with his wife, Denise Duhamel.

Mark Cox chairs the creative writing department at the University of North Carolina, Wilmington. His latest book is *Thirty-Seven Years from the Stone*. His honors include a Whiting Writers' Award, a Pushcart Prize, and fellowships from the Kansas Arts Commission and the Vermont Council on the Arts.

Jim Daniels's most recent books of poetry include *Night with Drive-by Shooting Stars* and *Digger's Blues*. Other poetry collections include *M-80, Blessing the House*, and *Blue Jesus*; short-story collections include *No Pets* and the forthcoming *Detroit Tales*. Daniels is also coeditor of the anthology *American Poetry: The Next Generation*.

Cortney Davis is the author of a memoir, *I Knew a Woman: Four Women Patients and Their Female Caregiver* and a collection of poems entitled *Details of Flesh*. She is also coeditor of two anthologies of creative writing by nurses, *Between the Heartbeats* and *Intensive Care*. Her honors include a National Endowment for the Arts Poetry Fellowship.

Karen Donovan's *Fugitive Red* won the Juniper Prize for poetry. A letterpress book designer for Oak City Press, she also writes about software and has edited science, social science, and business texts for the college market. She lives in Rhode Island and coedits the journal *Paragraph*.

Mark Doty is the author of six collections of poetry, most recently *Source* and *Sweet Machine*. *Atlantis* won a Lambda Literary Award, and *My Alexandria*, a National Book Award finalist, received the National Book Critics Circle Award and Britain's T. S. Eliot Prize. Doty has also published *Heaven's Coast: A Memoir* (winner of the PEN/Martha Albrand Award for First Nonfiction); an autobiography, *Firebird*; and a book-length essay, *Still Life with Oysters and Lemon*. Additional honors include fellowships from the Guggenheim, Rockefeller, and Whiting Foundations as well as the National Endowment for the Arts. He teaches at the University of Houston.

Amy Dryansky, the author of *How I Got Lost So Close to Home*, has published poems in the *Harvard Review, DoubleTake, Green Mountains Review*, and many other journals. Her honors include a grant from the Ludwig Vogelstein Foundation and a Pushcart Prize nomination. She lives in western Massachusetts, where she leads writing workshops for women and girls.

Denise Duhamel's most recent book is *Queen for a Day: New and Selected Poems.* Other works include *The Star-Spangled Banner, Kinky, Girl Soldier,* and *Smile!* With Maureen Seaton, she is the coauthor of *Exquisite Politics, Little Novels,* and *Oyl.* Her awards include a fellowship from the National Endowment for the Arts, and her poetry has been featured on NPR's *All Things Considered* and in Bill Moyers's PBS series *Fooling with Words.* She teaches at Florida International University.

Cornelius Eady's books include *Brutal Imagination, Victims of the Latest Dance Craze,* and *The Autobiography of a Jukebox.* He has received fellowships from the Guggenheim Foundation, the National Endowment for the Arts, the Rockefeller Foundation, and the Lila Wallace–Reader's Digest Foundation.

Heid Erdrich is the author of *Fishing for Myth,* a Minnesota Voices Project winner, and the recipient of a Minnesota Book Award. A Bush Leadership Fellow, she is also coeditor of the anthology *Sister Nations: Native American Women Writers on Community.* She teaches at the University of St. Thomas in St. Paul, Minnesota.

Martín Espada's latest book of poems is *A Mayan Astronomer in Hell's Kitchen.* He is also the author of *Imagine the Angels of Bread, City of Coughing and Dead Radiators,* and other volumes of poetry. He has edited *El Coro: A Chorus of Latino and Latina Poets* and *Poetry Like Bread: Poets of the Political Imagination.* His awards include the PEN/Voelker Award for Poetry, two fellowships from the National Endowment for the Arts, and a Massachusetts Artists Foundation fellowship. He teaches at the University of Massachusetts, Amherst.

Susan Firer's third book, *The Lives of the Saints and Everything,* won the Cleveland State University Poetry Center Prize and the Posner Award. Her most recent book, *The Laugh We Make When We Fall,* won the 2001 Backwaters Prize. Her work has appeared in many anthologies and reviews, including *The Best American Poetry.*

Amy Gerstler's most recent book of poems is *Medicine.* She is also the author of *Bitter Angel,* winner of a National Book Critics Circle Award, *Crown of Weeds,* and *Nerve Storm.* In addition to writing poetry, Gerstler writes fiction and essays.

Kate Gleason's work has been anthologized in *Best American Poetry, Boomer Girls,* and the *Yearbook of American Poetry,* among others. She is the author of two poetry chapbooks, *Making As If to Sing* and *The Brighter the Deeper.* Her awards include a New Hampshire State Council on the Arts fellowship, a New Hampshire Writer's Project Outstanding Emerging Writer Award, and a

National Endowment for the Arts fellowship. She has also served as a poet-in-the-schools and edited the literary arts journal *Peregrine*.

David Graham is the author of six poetry collections, most recently *Greatest Hits* and *Stutter Monk*. He is also coeditor of *After Confession: Poetry As Autobiography*, an anthology of essays on the topic of confessional poetry. His honors include an Academy of American Poets Award, and he has served as poet-in-residence at the Frost Place in Franconia, New Hampshire.

Bob Hicok is the author of *The Legend of Light* (winner of the Felix Pollack Prize in Poetry), *Plus Shipping*, and *Animal Soul*, a nominee for the National Book Critics Circle Award. His newest collection, *Insomnia Diary*, is forthcoming.

Tony Hoagland's first book, *Sweet Ruin*, won the Brittingham Prize in Poetry from the University of Wisconsin Press. *Donkey Gospel* received the Academy of American Poets' James Laughlin Award. Other awards include fellowships from the National Endowment for the Arts and the Provincetown Fine Arts Work Center. His poems and critical essays have also appeared widely, in such places as the *Gettysburg Review*, the *Harvard Review*, and *Ploughshares*.

Bob Holman's poetry collections include *The Collect Call of the Wild*, and he has edited three anthologies, including *Aloud! Voices from the Nuyorcian Poets Café*. Holman also produced *The United States of Poetry* for PBS, was part of MTV's *Spoken Word Unplugged*, and is currently editing *The World of Poetry* (worldofpoetry.org). The founder of Mouth Almighty Records, the first major label devoted to poetry, he is a visiting professor of Writing and Integrated Arts at Bard College and proprietor of the Bowery Poetry Club.

Janet Holmes is the author of *Humanophone*, *The Green Tuxedo*, and *The Physicist at the Mall*, which Joy Harjo selected for the Anhinga Prize. Her poems have twice been chosen to appear in editions of *The Best American Poetry*, and her awards include fellowships from the Bush Foundation, the McKnight Foundation, and the Minnesota State Arts Board. She teaches in the MFA program at Boise State University.

Ann Hostetler teaches English and creative writing at Goshen College in Indiana, where she lives with her husband and four children. She is the author of *Empty Room with Light*, a poetry collection, and the editor of *A Cappella: Mennonite Voices in Poetry*. Her work has appeared in a wide range of periodicals, from the *American Scholar* to *Mothering Magazine*.

Andrew Hudgins's most recent collection is *Babylon in a Jar*. His other works include the poetry collections *The Glass Hammer: A Southern Childhood* and *The Never-Ending* and a book of essays, *The Glass Anvil*. Among Hudgins's many honors are fellowships from the National Endowment for the Arts and the Ingram Merrill Foundation. He teaches at the University of Cincinnati.

Cynthia Huntington's *The Radiant* won the 2001 Levis Prize from Four Way Books. She is also the author of *The Fish-Wife*, *We Have Gone to the Beach*,

a Beatrice Hawley Award winner, and *The Salt House*, a prose memoir. Her
honors include fellowships from the National Endowment for the Arts, and
grants from the Massachusetts Arts Foundation and the New Hampshire State
Council on the Arts. A professor of English and the director of creative writing
at Dartmouth, Huntington also teaches in the MFA in writing program at
Vermont College.

Holly Iglesias is the author of *Hands-On Saints*. Her work has appeared in a
variety of journals, including the *Prose Poem*, *Crab Orchard Review*, and
Green Mountains Review. Her honors include a grant from the Massachusetts
Cultural Council and a Frank O'Hara Award for her chapbook *Good Long
Enough*. She is also coeditor of *His Hands, His Tools, His Sex, His Dress:
Lesbian Writers on Their Fathers* and *Every Woman I've Ever Loved: Lesbian
Writers on Their Mothers*.

Bruce Jacobs is the author of the nonfiction book *Race Manners: Navigating
the Minefield Between Black and White Americans* as well as a book of poems,
Speaking Through My Skin, which won the Naomi Long Madgett Award. He is
a Harvard graduate who has won writing residencies at the MacDowell Colony
and elsewhere. He lives in Baltimore.

Louis Jenkins's books include *The Winter Road*, *Just Above Water*, and *Nice
Fish*. His poems have been published in such journals as the *American Poetry
Review*, the *Kenyon Review*, and the *Paris Review* and have been anthologized
in *Literature: The Evolving Canon* and *The Rag Bone Shop of the Heart*. He has
been featured on *A Prairie Home Companion* and at the Geraldine R. Dodge
Poetry Festival. He lives in Minnesota.

Rodney Jones's most recent books of poetry are *Elegy for the Southern Drawl*,
Things That Happen Once, and *Apocalyptic Narrative*. His many honors include
a National Book Critics Circle Award, a Guggenheim fellowship, and awards
from the Academy of American Poets and the *Kenyon Review*. He teaches at
Southern Illinois University, Carbondale.

Allison Joseph is the author of *What Keeps Us Here*, *Soul Train*, and *In Every
Seam*. She has received a Woman Poets Series Competition Award, a John C.
Zacharias First Book Prize, and awards from the Illinois Arts Council. She
teaches at Southern Illinois University, Carbondale.

Julia Kasdorf's books of poetry include *Eve's Striptease* and *Sleeping Preacher*,
which won the 1991 Agnes Lynch Starrett Poetry Prize and the 1993 Great
Lakes Colleges Association Award. She is also the author of *The Body and the
Book: Writing from a Mennonite Life*, a collection of essays and poems. Her
poems have appeared in magazines such as the *New Yorker*, the *Paris Review*,
and *Poetry*, as well as in many anthologies. She teaches at Penn State
University.

Laura Kasischke's most recent poetry collections include *Dance and Disappear*,
winner of the Juniper Prize, *What It Wasn't*, and *Fire and Flower*. She is also

the author of three novels: *The Life before Her Eyes*, *White Bird in a Blizzard*, and *Suspicious River*. Her awards include a National Endowment for the Arts Fellowship and Hopwood Awards from the University of Michigan. She teaches at Washtenaw Community College in Michigan.

Josie Kearns is the author of *New Numbers* (poems) and the nonfiction book, *Life after the Line*. Her honors include grants from the Michigan Council for Arts and Cultural Affairs, a Cobden Fellowship, three Hopwood Awards, and the first MacLeod-Grobe Prize from *Poetry Northwest*. The coeditor of the anthology *New Poems from the Third Coast*, she teaches writing and literature at the University of Michigan.

Deborah Keenan's books include *Happiness* and *The Only Window That Counts*, as well as *Looking for Home: Women Writing about Exile* (coedited with Roseann Lloyd). She has received National Endowment for the Arts and Bush Foundation grants in addition to awards from the Loft-McKnight Foundation and the Minnesota State Arts Board. She teaches at Hamline University and is a core faculty member at the Loft, a Twin Cities center for writers.

Julie King is a poet and short-story writer whose work has appeared in a wide variety of journals including *Puerto Del Sol*, *Fiction International*, and *Cimarron Review*. She is also a filmmaker who wrote, directed, and produced the film *Worlds*. With her husband, Tom Dooley, she serves as poetry editor of *Eclectica* magazine and teaches at the University of Wisconsin Parkside.

Yusef Komunyakaa's books of poetry include *Talking Dirty to the Gods*; *The Pleasure Dome*; *Thieves of Paradise*, a National Book Critics Circle Award finalist; and *Neon Vernacular*, winner of the Kingsley Tufts Poetry Award and the Pulitzer Prize for Poetry. He has also coedited an anthology of jazz poetry and published a collection of prose entitled *Blues Notes*. He has received awards from the National Endowment for the Arts, and he received a Bronze Star for his service in Vietnam.

Norbert Krapf is the author of twelve poetry collections, including *Somewhere in Southern Indiana*, *Blue-Eyed Grass: Poems of Germany*, *Bittersweet along the Expressway: Poems of Long Island*, and *The Country I Come From*. Winner of the Lucille Medwick Memorial Award from the Poetry Society of America, he has directed the C. W. Post Poetry Center of Long Island University since 1985.

Laurie Kutchins's *Between Towns* won Texas Tech University Press's First Poetry Book Award, and her second collection, *The Night Path*, received the Isabella Gardner Poetry Award. Her poems have appeared in many journals and magazines, including *Ploughshares*, the *New Yorker*, and the *Kenyon Review*. She teaches creative writing at James Madison University in Virginia.

Dorianne Laux is the author of three books of poetry: *Awake*, *What We Carry* (a finalist for the National Book Critics Circle Award), and *Smoke*. She is also the coauthor, with Kim Addonizio, of *The Poet's Companion: A Guide to the Pleasures of Writing Poetry*. Her work has appeared in *The Best American Poetry* as well as in many journals, and her honors include a Pushcart Prize, a fellowship from the National Endowment for the Arts, and a Guggenheim Fellowship. She teaches in the University of Oregon's creative writing program.

Eleanor Lerman is the author of *The Mystery of Meteors, Armed Love,* and *Come the Sweet By and By.* A Juniper Prize winner, she also received a New York Foundation for the Arts grant for fiction writing. She lives in New York City.

Jan Heller Levi's *Once I Gazed at You in Wonder* won the 1998 Walt Whitman Award from the Academy of American Poets. She is also the editor of *A Muriel Rukeyser Reader* and is currently working on a biography of Rukeyser. She lives in New York City and in St. Gallen, Switzerland.

Lisa Lewis's *The Unbeliever* won the Brittingham Prize for Poetry. *Silent Treatment* won the National Poetry Series, selected by Stanley Plumly. A recipient of awards from the *American Poetry Review, Crazyhorse,* and the *Missouri Review,* Lewis directs the creative writing program at Oklahoma State University.

Timothy Liu's books include *Hard Evidence, Say Goodnight, Burnt Offerings,* and *Vox Angelica,* which won the Poetry Society of America's Norma Farber First Book Award. He is also the editor of *Word of Mouth: An Anthology of Gay American Poetry.* His poems have been widely anthologized and have appeared in such journals as the *Kenyon Review, Ploughshares,* and *Poetry.* He teaches at William Paterson University.

Rachel Loden is the author of *The Last Campaign* and *The Hotel Imperium,* winner of the University of Georgia Press's Contemporary Poetry Series and named one of the ten best poetry books of 2000 by the *San Francisco Chronicle Book Review.* Her poems have appeared in such journals as the *Antioch Review, New American Poetry,* and the *Paris Review,* as well as in *The Best American Poetry.* Her awards include a Pushcart Prize and a California Arts Council fellowship.

Monifa A. Love's recent books include *Freedom in the Dismal* and *My Magic Pours Secret Libations.* Her work has appeared in the *American Voice, African American Review, Essence,* and other magazines, and has also been anthologized in *In Search of Color Everywhere.* Love was the first woman to win the Zora Neale Hurston/Richard Wright Award for Creative Writing.

Thomas Lux's most recent book of poems is *The Street of Clocks.* Among his other collections are *New and Selected, Split Horizon,* and *Half Promised Land.* His many awards include fellowships from the National Endowment for the Arts and the Guggenheim Foundation and a Kingsley Tufts Award for *Split Horizon.* He teaches in the MFA programs at Sarah Lawrence College and Warren Wilson.

Rebecca McClanahan's most recent books are the essay collection *The Riddle Song and Other Rememberings* and the poetry collections *Naked As Eve* and *The Intersection of X and Y.* Her work has been widely anthologized and published in such journals as *Crazyhorse*, the *Kenyon Review*, and *Poetry*. She lives in New York City.

Paula McLain is the author of *Less of Her*. Her poems have appeared in journals such as the *Green Mountains Review*, *Third Coast*, and *Quarterly West*, and her honors include a fellowship from the National Endowment for the Arts.

Jane Mead is the author of *House of Poured-out Waters* and *The Lord and the General Din of the World*, a Whiting Writer's Award winner and winner of the Kathryn A. Morton Prize. She has received a Completion Grant from the Lannan Foundation and has published a chapbook version of a long poem entitled "A Truck Marked Flammable." She teaches at Wake Forest University.

Jeredith Merrin is the author of the poetry collections *Bat Ode* and *Shift*, as well as *An Enabling Humility: Marianne Moore, Elizabeth Bishop, and the Uses of Tradition*. She is a professor of English at Ohio State University.

Leslie Adrienne Miller's latest book of poems is *Eat Quite Everything You See*. Other collections include *Yesterday Had a Man in It* and *Ungodliness*. Her work has appeared in such journals as the *Harvard Review*, the *North American Review*, and *Crab Orchard Review*. She teaches at the University of St. Thomas in St. Paul, Minnesota.

Laurel Mills is the author of four books of poetry, including *I Sing Back* and *The Gull Is My Divining Rod*. Her poems have been published in such journals as *Ms.*, the *Kenyon Review*, and *Calyx*. She is also the author of the novel *Undercurrents*.

Kyoko Mori is the author of three novels—*Shizuko's Daughter*, *One Bird*, and *Stone Field, True Arrow*—a collection of poetry, *Fallout*; a memoir, *The Dream of Water*; and a book of essays, *Polite Lies*. Mori is currently a Briggs-Copeland lecturer in creative writing at Harvard.

Thylias Moss's books include *Last Chance for the Tarzan Holler*, *Small Congregations*, and *Rainbow Remnants in Rock Bottom Ghetto Sky*. Her awards include a MacArthur Fellowship, a Guggenheim Fellowship, a Witter Bynner Award for Poetry, and a Whiting Award. She is a professor of English at the University of Michigan.

Kel Munger's *The Fragile Peace You Keep* won the Minnesota Voices Project Award for Poetry. She is a former Pearl Hogrefe Fellow in Creative Writing at Iowa State University, and her poems and short stories have appeared in a number of journals. She lives in Sacramento, California.

David Mura's books of poetry include *After We Lost Our Way* and *The Colors of Desire*. He has also written two memoirs, *Turning Japanese* and *Where the Body Meets Memory*, as well as a collection of literary criticism entitled *Songs for Uncle Tom, Tonto, and Mr. Moto*. He lives in Minneapolis with his wife, Susan, his two sons, Nikko and Tomo, and his daughter, Samantha, who inspired "Listening" and who is now thirteen.

Kathleen Norris's books of poetry include *Little Girls in Church* and *Journey: New and Selected Poems 1969–1999*. Her nonfiction works include *The Virgin of Bennington*, *Dakota: A Spiritual Geography*, *Amazing Grace: A Vocabulary of Faith*, and *The Cloister Walk*.

William Olsen's most recent collection of poems is *Trouble Lights*. *The Hand of God and a Few Bright Flowers* was a National Poetry Series selection and a winner of the Texas Institute of Arts Poetry Award. He is also the author of *Vision of a Storm Cloud*. Awards include a National Endowment for the Arts fellowship, a YHMA/The Nation Discovery Award, and the *Poetry Northwest* Helen Bullis Award. He teaches at Western Michigan University.

John Reinhard is the author of two award-winning collections of poetry, *On the Road to Patsy Cline* and *Burning the Prairie*. He is the recipient of Hopwood Awards from the University of Michigan as well as a Bush Foundation grant and a Loft-McKnight fellowship. He lives in Fairbanks, Alaska, with his wife, Chris, and their children, Quinn and Matthew, and teaches at the University of Alaska in Fairbanks.

Louis Rodriguez's *Poems across the Pavement* won the Poetry Center Book Award from San Francisco State University, and his next collection, *The Concrete River*, won the PEN West/Josephine Miles Award for Literary Excellence. His memoir, *Always Running: La Vida Loca, Gang Days in L.A.*, received the Carl Sandburg Award of the Friends of the Chicago Public Library. Rodriguez, the founder of Tia Chucha Press, is also the author of a children's book, *América Is Her Name*.

Natasha Sajé's *Red under the Skin* won the Agnes Lynch Starrett Prize. Her poems, reviews, and essays appear in many journals, including the *American Voice*, *Poetry*, and *Ploughshares*, and her honors include the Barrister Writer-in-Residence at Sweet Briar College and grants from the Maryland State Arts Council. As well as serving on the MFA faculty at Vermont College, she is assistant professor of English and director of the Poetry Series at Westminster College in Salt Lake City.

Maureen Seaton's most recent book of poems is *Little Ice Age*. *Furious Cooking* won the Iowa Poetry Prize, preceded by *The Sea among the Cupboards* (a Capricorn Award winner) and *Fear of Subways*. With Denise Duhamel, she has also coauthored the collaborative poetry collections *Exquisite Politics*, *Oyl*, and *Little Novels*.

Diane Seuss is the author of *It Blows You Hollow*. Her work has appeared in such magazines as *Alaska Quarterly Review* and *Primavera*, and her awards include a Jewel Heart Poetry Prize. She has performed with Allen Ginsberg and Patti Smith at the University of Michigan's Hill Auditorium and teaches writing and literature at Kalamazoo College.

Betsy Sholl's most recent book, *Don't Explain*, was a Felix Pollack Award winner. She is also the author of *The Red Line* and three earlier collections. Sholl, the recipient of a National Endowment for the Arts Fellowship and a Maine Artists Fellowship, has taught in the Writing Program at MIT and currently teaches at the University of Southern Maine and in the MFA program at Vermont College.

Cathy Song's most recent collection of poems is *The Land of Bliss*. She is also the author of *School Figures*, *Picture Bride*, and *Frameless Windows, Squares of Light*. Her awards include a Yale Younger Poets Prize and a National Endowment for the Arts fellowship. She lives in Honolulu with her husband and three children.

Kate Sontag is the coeditor of *After Confession: Poetry As Autobiography*. Her poems have been published in a variety of journals, including *Prairie Schooner*, the *Green Mountains Review*, and the *Valparaiso Review*. Winner of the 1995 Ronald Bayes Poetry Prize from the *Sandhills Review*, she teaches at the University of Wisconsin Oshkosh.

Gary Soto's poetry collections include *New and Selected Poems*, a finalist for both the Los Angeles Times Book Award and the National Book Award. His many awards include the Discovery–The Nation Prize and the U.S. Award of the International Poetry Forum, as well as fellowships from the Guggenheim Foundation, the National Endowment for the Arts, and the California Arts Council. In 1999, he received the Literature Award from the Hispanic Heritage Foundation.

Marcia Southwick, the cofounder of the *Missouri Review* with Larry Levis, is the author of *The Night Won't Save Anyone* and *Why the River Disappears*. Her latest book of poems is *A Saturday Night at the Flying Dog*, which won the Field Poetry Prize. Southwick has taught at the University of Iowa Writers Workshop and the University of New Mexico in Albuquerque, as well as in the Warren Wilson MFA Program.

Virginia Chase Sutton is the author of *Netting the Gaudy Pearls*. Her work has appeared in many magazines, including the *Antioch Review*, the *Paris Review*, and *Ploughshares*. Her honors include fellowships from Bread Loaf and Writers at Work as well as a Paumanock Poetry Prize. She lives in Tempe, Arizona.

Alison Townsend is the author of two books of poetry, *What the Body Knows* and *The Blue Dress: Poems and Prose Poems*. Her work has been anthologized widely, and her poems and essays have appeared in such places as *Prairie Schooner*, *Calyx*, and the *Women's Review of Books*. She teaches at the University of Wisconsin Whitewater, as well as at In Our Own Voices, a private writing workshop for women.

Leslie Ullman's *Slow Work through Sand* won the Iowa Poetry Prize in 1997. She is also the author of *Dreams by No One's Daughter* and *Natural Histories*, winner of a Yale Younger Poets Award. A two-time National Endowment for the Arts Fellow, Ullman directs the creative writing program at the University of Texas, El Paso.

Judith Vollmer's full-length poetry collections are *The Door Open to the Fire*, winner of a Cleveland State Poetry Center Prize, and *Level Green*, winner of the Brittingham Prize. Other honors include a National Endowment for the Arts fellowship and a grant from the Pennsylvania Council on the Arts. Vollmer coedits the national poetry magazine *5 A.M.* and serves as director of the writing program at the University of Pittsburgh, Greensburg.

Ronald Wallace's most recent poetry collections are *Time's Fancy* and *The Uses of Adversity. Long for This World* is forthcoming. He is the codirector of the creative writing program at the University of Wisconsin Madison, and the poetry editor for the University of Wisconsin Press. He divides his time between Madison and his forty-acre farm in Bear Valley, Wisconsin.

Belle Waring is the author of *Dark Blonde*, which won the Levis Reading Prize, and *Refuge*. Her honors include fellowships from the National Endowment for the Arts, the D.C. Commission on the Arts, the Virginia Center for the Creative Arts, and the Fine Arts Work Center in Provincetown, Massachusetts. She holds university degrees in both English and nursing and has contributed commentary to National Public Radio.

Afaa Michael Weaver's books include *Multitudes: Poems Selected and New*, *The Ten Lights of God*, and *Talisman*. He is also the author of *These Hands I Know: African American Writers on Family*, an anthology of essays. Weaver is a playwright, fiction writer, and journalist whose honors include fellowships from the National Endowment for the Arts, the Pennsylvania Council on the Arts, and the Pew Charitable Trusts.

Charles Harper Webb's poetry collections include *Tulip Farms and Leper Colonies*; *Liver*, which won the 1999 Felix Pollack Prize; and *Reading the Water*, which won the S. F. Morse Poetry Prize and the Kate Tufts Discovery Award. He is also the editor of *Stand up Poetry: The Anthology*, and the coeditor of *Grand Passion: The Poets of Los Angeles and Beyond*. His honors include a Whiting Writer's Award and a fellowship from the Guggenheim Foundation.

Bruce Weigl's numerous books of poetry include *The Unraveling Strangeness*, *Archeology of the Circle: New and Selected Poems*, *Dien Cai Dau*, *What Saves Us*, *Sweet Lorain*, and *Song of Napalm*. He is also the author of a memoir, *The Circle of Hanh*, and the coauthor of *Poems from Captured Documents* (with Thanh T. Nguyen). His many honors include a fellowship from the National Endowment for the Arts and a Pushcart Prize, as well as a Bronze Star for his service in Vietnam.

Roger Weingarten's poetry collections include *Ghost Wrestling*, *Infant Bonds of Joy*, and *Shadow, Shadow*. He is also the coeditor of four poetry anthologies, including *Poets of the New Century* and *New American Poets of the '90s*, and the editor of *Ghost Writing: Haunted Tales by Contemporary Writers*. His awards include a Pushcart Prize, a National Endowment for the Arts Creative Writing Fellowship, and four Vermont Council on the Arts Individual Artist grants.

David Wojahn's most recent poetry collection is *Spirit Cabinet*. Other poetry volumes include *The Falling Hour*, *Late Empire*, and *Mystery Train*, and he is the author of a book of essays, *Strange Good Fortune*. His many honors include the George Kent Memorial Prize from *Poetry* magazine, fellowships from the National Endowment for the Arts and the Provincetown Fine Arts Work Center, the Yale Younger Poets Award, and the William Carlos Williams Book Award. He is a professor of English and the director of the program in creative writing at Indiana University, and a member of the MFA in writing faculty at Vermont College.

PERMISSIONS

INDEX